The

REAL GIRL
NEXT DOOR

The
REAL GIRL
NEXT DOOR

Denise Richards

GALLERY BOOKS

New York   London   Toronto   Sydney   New Delhi

Gallery Books
A Division of Simon & Schuster, Inc.
1230 Avenue of the Americas
New York, NY 10020

First Gallery Books paperback edition April 2012

Photo credits: Insert p. 6, top left: © Lara Porzak; all other photos courtesy
of the author

GALLERY BOOKS and colophon are registered trademarks
of Simon & Schuster, Inc.

For information about special discounts for bulk purchases,
please contact Simon & Schuster Special Sales at 1-866-506-1949
or business@simonandschuster.com

The Simon & Schuster Speakers Bureau can bring authors to
your live event. For more information or to book an event
contact the Simon & Schuster Speakers Bureau at 1-866-248-3049
or visit our website at www.simonspeakers.com.

Designed by Jaime Putorti

Manufactured in the United States of America

10   9   8   7   6   5   4   3

Library of Congress Cataloging-in-Publication Data

Richards, Denise
    The real girl next door / Denise Richards.
        p.   cm.
    ISBN-13: 978-1-4516-3321-4
    ISBN-10: 1-4516-3321-1
1. Richards, Denise, 1971–   2. Actors—United States—Biography.
3. Television personalities—United States—Biography.   I. Title.
    PN2287.R475A3   2011
    791.4302'8092—dc23
[B]   2011019745

ISBN 978-1-4516-3322-1
ISBN 978-1-4516-3323-8 (ebook)

This book is dedicated to my beautiful daughters, Sami and
Lola; my sister, Michelle (Nellie); my dad, Irv; and my late
mom, Joni, who continues to show me the way.

In loving memory, Joni Richards . . .

CONTENTS

....

25 Things You May Want to Know About Me Right Now

1. **Where am I right now?** *At home, with my laptop on my kitchen table.*

2. **What am I wearing?** *Jeans, white tank top, and sparkly flip-flops.*

3. **Where are my daughters?** *I don't know. Just kidding. They're here, working on art projects.*

4. **Do I talk to Charlie?** *Yes.*

5. **What would be my dream job?** *A role in a movie with Quentin Tarantino directing.*

6. **What's the best advice I've been given?** *My mom always told me that I'm a lot stronger than I think.*

7. **What's my favorite thing about myself?** *My patience.*

8. **What's my least favorite thing about myself?** *I'm a little stubborn.*

9. **What's my weirdest physical quality?** *I have flat feet.*

10. **What do I see when I look in the mirror that other people don't see?** *I think people see everything—and many have seen everything.*

11. **What's been my best idea?** *To see the world, starting when I was eighteen.*

12. **What's been my worst idea?** *Too many.*

13. **What would I change in other people?** *Their judgment.*

14. **What would I change about myself?** *To be less trusting.*

15. **When was the last time I cried?** *When one of my girls asked if her Nana—my mom—could see her from heaven.*

16. **How would I describe my senior high school yearbook photo?** *Totally '80s. My hair said it all.*

17. **My favorite cheesy song is . . .** *Journey's "Don't Stop Believing."*

18. **What's the one album I can't live without?** *Guns N' Roses's* Appetite for Destruction.

19. **Boxers or briefs on men?** *None.*

20. **What did I sleep in last night?** *A thong and a tank top.*

21. **If I'm upset . . .** *I'm very vocal.*

22. **Favorite place to travel?** *Anywhere tropical. I love the beach.*

23. **Question I'd ask Oprah?** *If I can have a personal tour of her Montecito home.*

24. **Every day I try to . . .** *live in the moment.*

25. **Tomorrow I will . . .** *try to get closer to where I need to be.*

INTRODUCTION

....

IF LIFE WERE a dance, what kind would yours be? Ballet? Modern? Country line? The twist? Salsa? Paso doble? A waltz? This came up recently in a conversation with a friend, and as much as I wish mine were a graceful ballet, I'm never going to be that perfect or practiced, and frankly, I don't care. If my life is more of an improvised two-step, with the emphasis on improvisation, so be it. That's my style—and one I think many people would recognize as their own.

You'd know what I'm talking about if you'd been with me lately. Over the past two months, I've made six trips to New York from my home in Los Angeles. That's a trip about every ten days. If nothing else, I'm adept at packing and unpacking, zipping through airport security, and running life from the two-inch screen of my iPhone and BlackBerry—yes, I have both. But like any other single working mother of two, my life is packed with so much more.

In the midst of all that travel, I dealt with school projects, packed lunches, and scheduled playdates; I rescued a dog, made valentines for school parties, set up my dad on one of his first dates since my mom passed away three years ago, auditioned for a couple TV pilots, guest-hosted two TV shows, signed an endorsement deal with a perfume company, nursed myself through a bout of bronchitis, made umpteen dinners, had several meetings with my contractor and designer about my home, which I'm remodeling, had meetings for other branding opportunities, launched a monthly pet adoption for Best Friends on *Access Hollywood*, turned forty, planned my daughter's seventh birthday party, and watched as my ex-husband, the father of my two little girls, imploded in a public spectacle that left me horrified, worried, and sad.

In *The Real Girl Next Door*, I talk about how I manage this and more. The cheat sheet is this: I do it just like you, day by day, hour by hour, and if necessary, minute by minute. It sounds like crisis management, but it's not. Taking life day by day and living in the moment are the clichés of self-improvement, but the approach really does let you handle more than you think is possible, especially when you feel as if the ceiling is caving in. I don't have a road map full of answers; rather, I am going to take you down the road I traveled as I grew up, glammed up, and ultimately grew into myself. As you'll find out, I don't think you find the answers in life as much as you figure out the questions to ask and muster the courage to move ahead during difficult and confusing times, confident that you can handle new challenges.

On my thirtieth birthday, a dear friend who'd already gone through her thirties sent me a gorgeous flower arrangement with a note that said, "The best is yet to come." I'll never forget that card. She was right. The best did come. I got married to a man who I thought was my everlasting soul mate and became a mother to two beautiful daughters. But then the bottom dropped out of that fantasy. Dolly Parton once said, "If you want the rainbow, you gotta put up with the rain," and let me tell you, there were times it felt like torrential downpours. I went through a difficult and humiliating divorce, moved out of my home, saw my public image tarnished and my career suffer, and then on top of everything, my mom was diagnosed with cancer and passed away. For three years, I was at rock bottom. Everything pretty much sucked.

As I went through the worst times of my life, I also experienced the best—being a new mom. Since then, I've accepted that you never know what's going to happen. I like that about life—not knowing what's around the corner. Of course, I always hope for the best, but even during the worst of times, I've found some good comes out of it.

Indeed, as my friend predicted in her birthday card, the best has come—in terms of self-confidence, motherhood, friendships, life lessons, and wisdom. I've learned to expect the unexpected and relish the days when the biggest emergency is when the kids are late for school. I know better than to get too comfortable, complacent, or upset. Nothing about being a mom is routine. But nothing about life is routine. When I look back at how I got to where I am today from my childhood in Downers Grove, Illinois, I don't see anything I'd describe as routine, normal, or predictable. It's been a wild ride.

In *The Real Girl Next Door*, I've written the book I wish that I'd had on my nightstand the past eight years. It's full of stories that I would've wanted to hear from a friend, the kind that could reassure me I'd get through my problems, too. As you'll see, I've tried to share not just what I've been through, but more important, how I've gotten through it all. Although most people reading this will already be familiar with the headlines, they won't know how I felt as everything happened, and in some cases, how I survived.

Not that my life is any more special or harder than anyone else's. No, I think the reality is that my experiences are similar to yours, spanning the gamut of good times, magical times, hard times, terrible times, and times when I rekindled hope after it seemed permanently gone. While there's no one way to live your life, all of us go through similar rites of passage, and I've always been someone who's interested in the ways each of us deal. I don't care about the *what happened* as much as I do the *what have I learned* and *what's next*.

I'm pragmatic in that way. I'm a great person to have around in a crisis. As you'll find out, I don't pass judgment and don't hold grudges. Clear-eyed and calm, I move forward. I don't always know where I'm going. Nor is what I want to accomplish always easy. But I've learned that if I'm open and honest with myself and others; if I ask enough people for advice; if I'm not afraid to face the truth; and if I put aside any fear of failure—I'll be able to figure things out, and usually end up where I need to be, which isn't always where I intended to go.

Hopefully, you're nodding your head. But you'll see as much when I explain how a shy, midwestern girl from a middle-class family who thought she'd be married forever and pop out a houseful of babies ended up a single mom whose trips to the grocery store are chronicled by paparazzi and splattered across the Internet. Some of that I would gladly trade, but for the most part, I like where I ended up and hope I'm pointed in the right direction for the future.

That's the goal here—to like yourself and be ready to face the day. I work at that all the time. Even as I think I have a grip on my agenda of kids, family, career, friendships, love, and feeling good inside and out, the deck gets shuffled. I don't need Freud to analyze why I've taken on such a huge project by myself in remodeling my home. A lot of my friends were surprised, and even my dad thought it was a big endeavor for a single working woman with two daughters. But that's who I am. When I make a decision, no matter how big or small, I stick to it and just do it. If I run into challenges along the way, I figure it out. I've learned to not live by the "what ifs" and not always worry about the outcome. I think that's a good quality and maybe sometimes not so good. I always follow my heart and my gut. I have an ex-boyfriend who thought perhaps I should think things through more when making decisions. He thought I was nuts tackling such a big project with my home (I mean, I gutted the damn thing), but he'll see when it's done that I was able to do it on my own. What was I gonna do? Wait until husband number two arrives to help me? Nope. I don't know when that will be and I want my house done! Home improvement. Self-improvement. What's the difference? If you overheard me on the phone, you wouldn't be able to tell if I was talking about the house or me. The questions are the same: What's good? What should I keep? What should I lose? What do I need to fix? Is it even fixable?

When my mother was nearing the final stages of her battle

with cancer, she knew the challenges I was going through, and she also saw how frightened I was about losing her. But she reassured me that I was much stronger than I knew, and in looking back, it turned out she was right. What did she see that I didn't? What did she know that I had to find out? I've come to realize it was my honesty. I called this book *The Real Girl Next Door* for a reason. I'm real, as in a real person, as in real honest, as in just plain real. I don't carry around a lot of clutter—at least I try not to. If I love someone, the person knows it. If I'm feeling passionate, it's going to be *some* time in the bedroom. If I have a problem, people will know about it. The only things about me that are fake are my boobs, but I'm real about that, too. I live to be that way.

When I was a Bond girl, I was prepped on what I said on TV and in interviews. It didn't matter what question was asked, I was supposed to answer in a way that would have the broadest appeal and try to come off as an accessible girl next door. I was to downplay questions asked about my racy role in *Wild Things* and try to come up with an intelligent side of my character. Intelligent? I was a Bond girl running around in hot pants! But okay! Everyone was supposed to perceive me a certain way, and therefore like the film. It was like answering staged questions in a beauty pageant. And it never felt right.

Like it or not, I'm someone who tells the truth. I was raised that way. At times I've kept my mouth shut rather than letting loose. I do believe in always telling the truth, but I also believe there is a time and a place for when. Being truthful is healthy, and it allows you to live with a clean conscience. I've found the more I'm my authentic self, the better off I am when it comes time to make decisions. I never thought I'd get divorced, but once I made the decision, I knew it was the right one for my children and me. I've learned I'd much rather be honest and like myself and where I am in my life than worry about everyone else liking me.

All that said, do I always know what I'm doing? No. Do I think I sometimes know what I'm doing? Yes. However, as you'll learn, though I take on too much and spread myself thin, I always put my children first. I have to remind myself that it's okay to devote a little time for me. Right before all of my recent trips to New York, I'd finally gotten myself back into shape, physically and emotionally. Embracing single, working mommyhood, I'd figured out how to manage carpooling my daughters, helping with homework, overseeing a huge remodel of my house, deal with all our dogs and the animal rescue I'm involved with, revamp my website, stay up on Twitter, have a social life with my friends, expand my brand, go on the occasional date, and travel.

On my last trip to New York, in mid-February 2011, I got on the plane thinking, "Finally, I've got things under control. Life is calm." I settled in with my decorating magazines and book and thought about my schedule. I was walking in the Red Heart fashion show and having dinner afterward with my friend Lisa Rinna and several other women. This is where I'm sure you moms (and dads!) can relate. I had a couple free days after the fashion show. I easily could have filled those days up instead of flying back home only to get back on the plane a couple days later. But I decided to head back home to be with my girls for those couple of days. My daughters were having Valentine's Day parties at school and it was important for me to be there. After the parties, I stayed the weekend and headed back to New York. My fortieth birthday was the next day, and I was filling in for Sherri Shepherd on *The View*.

I was nervous about sitting with Barbara, Whoopi, Joy, and Elisabeth. Although it was agreed beforehand that they wouldn't ask any questions about Charlie, I worried about other breaking celebrity news. I knew I had no control over anything that might happen, but I didn't want to be in a position where I was asked to comment on someone else's life, especially someone I might not know. Having previously been that person in the news, I knew how hurtful it was to hear the speculation and the half-truths about your personal life, and if the reports were true, it was even more painful. But for the first time in ages, I was in a good place; things were quiet and calm in the press with my personal life, and I was actually looking forward to being a cohost for *The View*.

Then I got off the plane at JFK International Airport and checked my phone. My voice mail was full and I had more than a hundred e-mails, text messages, and tweets. My community of Twitter followers keep me apprised of every bit of news, good and not so good, and when I saw what had happened, that Charlie had called in to the Dan Patrick radio show and unloaded some of his frustration about work, I said, "Oh, shit. I'm going on *The View* tomorrow." I had no idea what Charlie was thinking when he decided to do such an explosive interview about his job, but that's his business and has nothing to do with me. Or does it? We'd been in the kind of stable place I'd hoped to find. But his timing was impeccable as far as it concerned affecting my life and the girls. I wasn't at home to shield the children, and the next morning I found myself in the hallway of a show whose lifeblood was controversy, celebrity, and news. I'd walked into the eye of the perfect storm. The show had made a promise to me that they would not ask me any questions about Charlie. Of course, I'd made the commitment to the show three weeks prior to the air date, and I of all people know what amount of shit can happen in three weeks. Even so, I hoped they'd stick to their agreement about not asking me any questions about him and that damn radio interview. But I felt like a deer caught in headlights. As it turned out, my fears weren't unfounded.

Moments before we went live on the air, while I was getting touch-ups to my hair and makeup, there was a knock on my dressing room door. It was Barbara Walters and one of the show's producers. They said they had to ask me a couple of questions about Charlie. Otherwise, they would look foolish. Personally I would've rather they looked foolish but I understood their issues of credibility. But we had an agreement. My publicist, who was also present, asked what I wanted to do. With the clock ticking, and Barbara, the producer, and my publicist staring at me, I had a choice. Part of me was pissed off at being put in the situation, but another part of me realized that this was like thousands of other moments in life. I could get up and leave. I could argue and insist they live up to the agreement we'd made. Or I could grit my teeth, adapt to the new situation, and see what happened.

I'm sure you've found yourself in situations like this one, maybe not with Barbara Walters standing inches away as she waited for your decision, but one where you were uncomfortable, didn't want to be there, and wished it would all go away. Yet you know what you have to do, what you're going to do; you just don't know how you're going to do it. As I said, life doesn't come with an instruction book. There's your way. There's my way. And then there's that improvised two-step we often rely on. We take a chance and figure things out as we go. We learn from our mistakes. We laugh, we cry, we love, we fall down, and we get back up again. Sometimes I have no idea why we get back up again, but we do. And then we laugh again. We cry again. And we love again.

Welcome to my life.

PART ONE

·

Home Is
Where the
Heart Is

AS WITH ANYONE, to understand me, you have to know my family and how I was raised, and also understand that family has always meant everything to me, and still does. The way I was raised is a major reason why I've taken such offense to the slams I've received in the media from people who've never met me. I grew up in a nonjudgmental home. I remember being out with my mom when I was a little girl and pointing to a kid with grungy clothes and holes in his shoes, one of those "eww, look at that" moments, and my mom quickly shushed me, explaining that you don't make fun or pass judgment on other people. His family might not be able to afford new clothes and shoes, she said. There might've been other circumstances, too. I understood and learned a lesson that's stayed with me forever. Even though we didn't have much money, I immediately felt bad and wanted to help.

I learned at an early age that it doesn't matter what people look like or what their shortcomings may be, or how much or little money they have. I was raised to treat everyone equally and to treat someone how I would like to be treated. I needed few reminders, thanks to my relatives. I had a cousin who was deaf, one who was developmentally disabled, one who was gay, an uncle who lost his left leg, a grandpa who had a hook in lieu of a hand, a second cousin on my dad's side who went through a sex change and became a woman, an aunt who committed suicide, an uncle who was a recovering drug addict, and a grandma whose best friends were twin dwarfs.

This grandmother of mine ran a tavern in Wisconsin. We went there numerous times every summer. It was an eight-hour drive from where we lived in Illinois. Her place, called Lehmann's Pub, was next to a lake where we fished and caught bullfrogs. In the afternoon and at night, we darted in and out of the bar, which shared a kitchen with the house. We got to serve draft beer, which we loved, to see who could get the least foam. Imagine not even being a teenager and pouring beer? We were allowed one candy bar from the counter a day. My cousins used to stay there with us, too. With all the alcohol and cigarettes at the pub, it's amazing none of us ever dabbled in all that, but we didn't. The dwarf twins—about eighty years old—were regulars. They were sweet, adorable men, who also had a dwarf sister. I loved talking to them, they were so nice to my sister and me. My mom had known them when she was a little girl, and one time I asked if they'd always been that way. "No, they used to be younger," she said.

That was my mom. She was the smartest, strongest woman I've ever known. Even though my daughters, Sam and Lola, are in first grade and kindergarten right now, in many situations, I'll wonder if I'm being the same kind of sane, strong, tough, stable, and loving role model that my mom was for me. So much of who we become as adults is based on the parenting we received as children. My mom set a high bar, and I don't think it's that she always knew what she was doing. In fact, as she later confided, much of her parenting was based on trial and error, asking other moms how they did things, and simply being unafraid to be a parent rather than a friend.

From a family of five kids, she had a brother and three sisters, and I was the beneficiary of all the people skills she acquired from growing up in a large family. My mom was best friends with my dad's sister, and at fourteen, she met my dad, who was then eighteen and drafted. After serving two and a half years in the Vietnam War, he returned home and they fell in love. I don't think they spent a day apart ever again until my mom passed away. At sixteen she got pregnant with me, and on August 1, 1970, shortly after her seventeenth birthday, they exchanged vows in the local courthouse. On that same day, in the same courthouse, her parents' divorce was finalized.

I was born on February 17, 1971, and eighteen months later, my sister, Michelle, arrived. At times we were best friends, and other times we pounded the crap out of each other. We were one grade apart and had a lot of the same friends. We lived in Mokena, Illinois, in a tiny nine-hundred-square-foot, two-bedroom house. After my dad fixed it up, it was twelve hundred square feet. Soon after he finished, we moved to Downers Grove so he could be closer to his job with the phone company and spend more time at home with the family and my sister and I could go to better schools. My parents always put a premium on family time. My dad was home every night for dinner at six, and our weekends always involved family-oriented activities. My parents reserved one evening a week for themselves. Date night.

Unable to afford a home in Downers Grove right away, we

lived in a two-bedroom condo while my parents saved up for a house. After two years, they found a hundred-year-old fixer-upper, though that sounds even better than it was. The place needed major TLC. I was embarrassed when we first moved in. It was the ugliest house in the neighborhood, and I didn't want to live in an old place that needed so much work. Over time, it became a beautiful home. My parents did all the work themselves. They couldn't afford to pay a contractor. Nor did they want to. Every day after work my dad strapped on his tool belt and sawed and hammered away. My mom helped and did the decorating. They were a team in this effort to not merely reclaim the house, but to transform it into a shared vision.

Though thirty-some years have passed since that experience, it still stands out to me as a powerful primer on marriage, in real terms and metaphorically. My parents built something together: a house, a family, and a life. Tired, pinching pennies, breathing sawdust, they walked the talk, as the saying goes.

Whether or not they realized it, my parents were people who taught us daily to find worth and joy in people and life on the inside. As one who is not adverse to some retail therapy when I need a pick-me-up after a tough day, I appreciate the lessons they drummed into me from an early age: Money can't buy happiness. Makeup and expensive clothes don't make anyone more attractive. Judge people for the way they behave, not for what they say. All are truisms that ended up preparing me for a life in Hollywood by drumming into me one basic rule: "be real; know yourself, and be true to that."

I'm sure I frustrated my mom because from an early age I was a girly girl who loved looking through the fashion magazines and ached to wear makeup, which I was prohibited from doing until I was sixteen. Earlier than that, my mom thought girls wearing mascara, blush, and lipstick were just too young. "What's the rush?" she used to say. She wanted us to grow up first, develop, and get to know ourselves, inside and out, before we tried to change or enhance our appearance. As a mom, I couldn't agree more. I say bravo. I can already sense the pressures on my girls—and they're still babies, relatively speaking.

By junior high, though, I was sneaking lipstick out in my purse and applying it so heavily that one day a boy came up to me and said, "Kissing you would be like kissing a crayon." My mom wasn't averse to dressing up. I have some old photos of her with my dad in the mid and late 1970s, and she looked hot for their date nights. I loved watching my mom put her makeup on every day. She always looked beautiful and I still remember what her perfume smelled like.

Soon after my sister was born, my mom lost all of her hair. She was diagnosed with alopecia, a not uncommon condition that generally causes people to lose hair in small patches. In my mom's case, she lost all the hair on her head. Despite numerous exams, doctors were never able to explain why. It was a mystery. Not that it mattered. My mom was bald. Imagine, a beautiful young woman suddenly finding herself at nineteen years old without the thick mane of blond hair that had been such a defining part of her looks.

And it didn't grow back as the doctors said it would. Not after a year or two. Not for ten years. My mom wore wigs every day. She had a number of them, which of course my sister and I put on when we played dress-up. But they weren't the $5,000, high-quality, expensive wigs that looked real. My parents couldn't afford those, and I'm sure my mom was self-conscious about the way wigs looked on her, though as far as I remember, she never made a point of it. She always wore those wigs and scarves. If it bothered her, I never knew about it. That's just the way she was.

I spoke about the condition with my mom only a couple times, once when I was in my twenties and another time when she was sick with cancer. On both occasions she admitted that at first she'd been devastated, but then, with a shrug, she said, "What are you going to do? It was gone. I felt healthy in every other way and so it didn't matter. There were more important things to focus on."

2

WHEN WE LIVED in Mokena, we had a German short-haired pointer named Brutus. He was my dog. The two of us were inseparable, and one morning when I went into the backyard to give him my leftovers from breakfast, I couldn't find him. Panicked, I ran through the house, the front yard, and into the neighbors' yards, calling his name, without any luck. It turned out that my parents, anticipating our move to Downers Grove, had given him away. They said he needed a home where he had more room to run, and they found a nice family that lived on a farm outside of town. I was crushed. They hadn't told me. They hadn't even let me say good-bye. I cried for weeks. It was very tough love.

As cruel as I thought that was, my parents were practical and knew we were headed to a condo, where Brutus wouldn't have the kind of room to run that he required. My parents thought it would've been easier on me to tell me after the fact. In hindsight, my dad said they wished they had let me say good-bye to him and meet the family that was taking him. My mom was an animal lover, though. When she grew up, her family bred Irish setters, and once we settled into our Downers Grove house, she got another dog, a schnauzer named Strudel. Strudel was a rescue dog who was badly abused and blind in one eye, and when I asked my mom why she'd picked a one-eyed dog who was extremely timid from having been abused, she said, "Honey, she needed a good home."

Check. Another lesson that made a long-lasting impression. I loved that my mom didn't care if the dog was perfect or a pure-bred. In fact, the opposite was true; she wanted to get a dog that was hard to place. Strudel ended up living to be twenty-one. We also rescued a second schnauzer, another girl, which we named Gidget. My mom always wanted to open an animal sanctuary, but she got too sick. As a natural when it came to nurturing children and pets, she would've been great, given my soft spot for pets. With many dogs at my house now, and the rescue work I do, my mom and I would've had an amazing sanctuary. One day I will build one for her.

When I was a kid, we went camping in lieu of fancy vacations. I'm not talking about parking a motor home in a campsite. We camped with tents, sleeping bags, cookouts, and large spray cans of Off! bug repellent for the mosquitoes. Aside from fun and family time, I got to see how capable my parents were. My mom packed the coolers with all the food, and my dad was in charge of everything else. When we got to the campsite, he put up the tent, got a fire going in the pit, and set up the portable cooktop. My dad could do anything, whether it was putting on a new roof at home or turning a patch of ground in the woods into a cozy campsite.

I loved those trips, but I have to tell you, they made me appreciate the fancy hotels I enjoy now. My sister still goes camping with her family, though, and both of us still reminisce about swimming in lakes and roasting marshmallows at night after a day of hiking and canoeing.

I secretly loved when it rained so hard that we had to check into a local motel or, if we splurged, a hotel. Room service was out of the question. My sister and I always begged to have it, but it was too expensive. Instead, we always ate at an inexpensive coffee shop. Even though I imagined that the food from room service tasted better, I never went hungry or unsatisfied, and truth be told, the crayons and coloring books that many of those coffee shops gave to kids when we sat down were my favorite part of the meals.

As a kid, the simplest things amused me, such as catching lightning bugs or building a fort in the backyard. Riding my bike to a friend's house, neighborhood block parties, cookouts, ice-skating on the lake next to my grandmother's house—these were the activities that I loved to do. Now, my kids are so scheduled I keep a calendar just for their activities and lessons, and I know that's not unusual. But I can remember my mom simply saying, "Go see if so-and-so can play," and I'd get on my bike and ride to a friend's house, knock on the door, and see if they wanted to play. There was no setting up frickin' play dates! What happened to us?

I sound as if I'm dredging up memories of a bygone past, but life was simpler in our homey neighborhood where everyone knew each other. Then, it was safe for kids to ride down the street by themselves. My sister and I and our dad belonged to a father-daughter group called the Drifters, which gave us quality time alone with our dad. Once a month, we got together with a group of other girls and their dads and went on weekend trips. Depending on the season, we went canoeing, river rafting, cross-country skiing, and downhill skiing. At night, we stayed in cabins—girls in one, dads in another.

On one river trip, I pulled over to pee and went in the bushes. A short time later, I started to feel sick, and by nighttime, I had spots everywhere. One of the other dads was a doctor, but, as he said, you didn't need to be an MD to see the problem. It was poison ivy. On my butt! Not a good place to get it. And a little embarrassing when I had to show the dad who was the doctor my tush.

Downers Grove was a charming little town with cobblestone streets and cute mom-and-pop stores. There was one movie theater, where I saw *E.T.* and *Star Wars.* On summer nights, we walked to Bogg's ice cream, which to this day had the best homemade ice cream I've ever eaten. My parents took my sister and me to church on Sundays, and both of us attended CCD classes one day a week after school. We made our Communion and Confirmation.

Though we had our own rooms, Michelle and I did everything together, from gymnastics to pom-poms in junior high.

Both of us had a crush on Rob Lowe, we had a poster of him in our room, and we never missed an episode of *The Facts of Life*. I was always supportive of my sister, until she got her period before me. How could that be? I was so envious because I'd heard your boobs start to develop after you get your period, and now Michelle was getting a head start. I got my period the next year; my boobs never developed, and that would turn into a whole other story years later.

3

LOOKS DID MATTER. I'm not going to lie. There is so much pressure on girls and it sure starts young. Any girls who wanted to be like Blair on *The Facts of Life* had a vision of themselves with thick, long hair, nice, fashionable clothes, and makeup, and I have to plead guilty on all counts. But my fantasies of turning heads as I waltzed through the school cafeteria were tempered all through seventh and eighth grade by a nasty little girl who delighted in tormenting me. She called me Fish Lips and Unibrow, which gives you all the explanation you need to picture what I looked like during those awkward years (think skinny, overbite, and caterpillar eyebrows), and made my walking through the locker-filled hallways at school an emotional minefield.

I had good friends who rallied around and buoyed me when I broke down, while my mom, apparently able to see something in me that I didn't, advised me to be patient and wait for things to change. Braces helped, and at the end of eighth grade, I walked out of my final orthodontist appointment with a brand-new sparkling smile.

By fourteen, I was boy crazy. (Sorry, Mom!) My parents forbid me to date until I was sixteen, but with a short climb from my bedroom window to my bicycle, I managed to sneak out of the house regularly. I was also caught more often than not, thanks to my sister's willingness to snitch. There was a period when I was grounded for at least three-quarters of the year. But Michelle got her comeuppance a few years later. One night, a couple guys were knocking on my bedroom window in the middle of the night thinking they were going into her room. Assuming they were burglars, I screamed. That brought my dad, who arrived wielding a gun. By then, the guys had scrambled back out and were long gone. My sister told me in the morning that they were her friends—and no, I never snitched on her.

A year later, Michelle was caught sneaking out at night. As punishment, my dad removed her bedroom door. Shocked and horrified, we watched as he carried it into the garage. Then we laughed our asses off. It's even funnier all these years later, though my dad insists he'd do it all over again.

Both of my parents were strict. While I may not have appreciated it while growing up, I am grateful now that they had rules, and stuck to them. I do that with my girls. There's nothing more painful than watching them pout and fume when they have a time-out, but children want and need boundaries and parameters, and they want to know their parents care. My mom was direct when it came to talking to us about sex. It was what you'd expect from someone who was a teen mom herself. She was matter-of-fact, and rather than tell us to wait, she emphasized the consequences of being sexually active, explaining we'd better make damn sure we were serious about a boy before we had sex, and being responsible.

I heard her loud and clear, but I didn't have a boyfriend. I was content to bide my time until I could date. Meanwhile, I made the Tinley Park High cheerleading squad as a freshman, and I was looking ahead to being a sophomore as the year when my entire life would come together: I'd be a cheerleader, old enough to get my driver's license, old enough to date, and finally able to wear makeup. Notice the missing concern: academics. I was a solid A-B student who could've done better. Drama was one of the classes where I did achieve outstanding marks. I always came to life when we read and performed plays.

We didn't have a big theater department that put on annual school plays, but if we had, I'm sure I would've gone out for it. When I stepped into a character, even if we were just reading a play in class, I found it fun and exciting to get outside of myself and try to create the nuances of another person. I didn't have the tools or life experience I'd bring to the job later, but I had a willing, outgoing attitude, so whatever emotion was required, whether it was laughter, tears, or love, I did my best and went for it.

As I looked ahead to tenth grade, I saw myself as poised to blossom. All of the hurts and hardships of adolescent awkwardness, at least from the vantage of my perch at age fifteen, seemed to be safely disappearing in the rearview mirror. Indeed, as I skipped into the future, life could not have been set up any better for me. However, as I'd repeatedly find out over the years, every time you think you have life aced, something causes the ground to shift, dust to fly, and your head to spin; and that's what happened to me.

It was a first for me, and though I sound melodramatic now, back then I was only fifteen, and everything having to do with dating, cheerleading, appearances, and social standing involved melodrama. To be real, as in real honest, it was that time in your life when every matter seemed like life or death and I didn't know how I was going to survive.

So embarrassing, looking back. But true.

4

....

MY DAD WORKED for Illinois Bell, the phone company, climbing power poles and repairing broken or downed wires. It was hard but good, dependable work, and for the eight or nine months of the year the weather was nice or tolerable, so was the job. But the Chicago winters are extremely harsh, some of the worst in the country, especially when the wind whips up and drives the freezing temperatures even lower, and in those conditions, my dad's job sucked.

One weekend in the dead of winter while viewing a *Battle of the Network Stars* special, he watched enviously as the celebrities ran around in shorts and T-shirts. He called my mom into the room and pointed it out, as he did the sunshine, the palm trees, and the stars in their swimming suits. Yes, it was mid-

January, and they were swimming in Southern California. For
the next couple of months, he started every day by opening the
newspaper and checking the temperatures in Los Angeles and
San Diego. Then he compared them to Chicago.

As far as he was concerned, there was no comparison. Sunshine versus snow? Forget it. He wanted to move. If my mom
had been adamantly opposed to uprooting the family and leaving the house they had painstakingly remade, my sister and I
wouldn't have known. They were a team, and they made the
decision to move our family. I know it was hard for her, given
we could drive in any direction and eventually run into family
or friends. To her, Southern California had little to offer other
than warmer weather. But she was supportive of my dad, and
for my dad, who knew the pain of being pelted by razor-sharp
sleet while working atop a telephone pole, that was more than
enough.

Soon my parents flew out west and scoured Southern California for a nice, affordable place to raise two teenage girls. After
a week, they returned and explained they'd found an area they
liked near the ocean, a little surfing village called Oceanside.
With my dad carrying the conversation, I looked at my mom
and I was getting upset; I did not want to move to California.
I ran to my bedroom, slammed the door, and fell onto my bed.
For the first time, but not the last, I thought my life was over.

I wasn't alone. My sister didn't want to go, either (as an adult
I learned that my mom also wasn't crazy about the move, but I
love how she supported my father and never showed her true
feelings about it in front of us). That summer, with my dad having landed a job with a telephone start-up and full of the promise

of a better quality of life for all of us, we traveled to Oceanside. We packed our belongings, sold our house, and traded our faux-fur-lined winter coats for flip-flops. However, it was anything but paradise. Because home prices were beyond our reach, we moved into an apartment that was smaller than our old house. Then, to complicate matters, my dad's new company hit hard times and paychecks were unreliable.

As tension rose and the dinner table conversation somehow always tended toward the stability we'd left behind, Michelle and I tried out for the cheerleading team, and only one of us was selected. I would've preferred both of us had been chosen, but when it wasn't me, I was devastated and wanted to get on the next plane to Chicago, which, of course, wasn't possible.

But the situation hit rock bottom one day when I came home and didn't see the car parked out front. My mom avoided my questions, but once my dad came home, the truth came out. Our car had been repossessed. I'll never forget the look on my dad's face as my mom broke the news to him. He turned white and seemed for the first time in my life incredibly vulnerable, and that made a severe impression on me. It was one thing to mope like a self-centered teenager missing her friends, but entirely different to see someone you loved and cared about appear as wounded as my dad did that evening.

He had withstood months of us bashing his decision to move, and I have no idea of the criticism he heard from my mom in private, but he finally looked as if he couldn't take any more. His spirit was nearly broken, and as we knew, his self-confidence was already cracked, and I hated seeing that in my dad. Over the next few weeks, I overheard talks he had with my mom where he questioned his decisions and beat himself up pretty good. It hurt me to know that he was suffering. I wondered how much I'd contributed to his pain.

At that point, something in me snapped and suddenly I began to see things not just from my selfish point of view but also from his vantage, too. I didn't understand it as well as I do now, but I saw the risk my dad had taken in getting a new job, moving us to Oceanside, and hoping to create a more comfortable life for all of us, and as I thought about what it must have taken to make that decision, to actually roll the dice, I admired him more than ever. The first eight months hadn't worked out, but we weren't finished. If you looked at it another way, we were, in fact, still just getting started.

Following this epiphany, I had several long, emotional conversations with my mom and sister, and all of us agreed we had to do something to make my dad feel better. We all promised to do something in our own way. Mine was straightforward. I sat next to him one night as he watched TV, gave him a hug, and said, "Dad, I know you've been worrying about us. Don't worry anymore. We're going to get through this." I let him know that I was back on the team. "I know it's hard, but Mom and Michelle and I all talked, and we'll make it work."

We did. My mom got a job as an accountant at Albertsons grocery store, and soon I was hired there, too, as a bagger. When the boss found out I was underage, he let me go, but not before telling me that they'd hire me again after I turned sixteen. Sure enough, a few months later, I got my job back. In the interim, though, I'd gotten into long, acrylic fingernails, which slowed my productivity considerably. I fared better at my next job as a scooper at the local ice cream parlor. The owners hired cute girls, and it was packed with boys. Say no more, right?

The situation didn't get easier for my dad, who continued to struggle. My sister and I gave part of our paychecks to our dad, and with my mom pitching in financially, bills got paid, our car was returned, and with better attitudes all around, some of the guilt he shouldered lightened, and the sparkle returned to his eyes. That was the man I knew and loved and wanted to see happy. I rejoiced when I saw him hold hands with my mom as they went for a walk. Don't get me wrong, it was better to have job security and financial solvency than not, and I missed my old friends, as well as opportunities I might've had, such as being a cheerleader, but complaining and sulking didn't get us anywhere but down. It was more important to band together and have a home filled with love. I learned to value what I needed, not what I wanted, and I think all of us got a heavy dose of that during our first year in California.

After that first year, something remarkable happened. My mom's hair began to grow back. Miraculously and mysteriously, her alopecia disappeared. Doctors were unable to explain it. We thought it might've been the year-round sunshine and change in climate, but no one ever figured it out. One day, with her thick hair just above her shoulders, she donated her wigs to charity, and in doing so she made a statement that resonated with all of us. We were now home, starting a new chapter of our lives. My dad had taken a big risk in moving across country, and while it took longer than anticipated for some parts to work out, there were other benefits, such as my mom's hair. There would be more, too. My entire life would've been different if not for my dad's vision of raising his family in the sunshine.

Every day entails decisions involving incertitude and risk. Do I take a job? Do I go on a blind date? Do I live in a neighborhood that's convenient for me, or do I move where the schools are better for my girls? My whole life has involved risks that I may never have taken if not for the security my family provided with their support and love, the self-confidence my mom nurtured from an early age, and of course the example my dad offered in courage to go for what you believe will make you happy.

It's fascinating to look back on this now, because I've put my girls in similar situations, though they're younger. In creating a new, postmarried life, I had to take certain calculated risks, and I don't know if I would've done them as readily if not for the precedent my dad set. I got the confidence I needed as a woman from my mom, and my dad gave me the courage to endure and carry on.

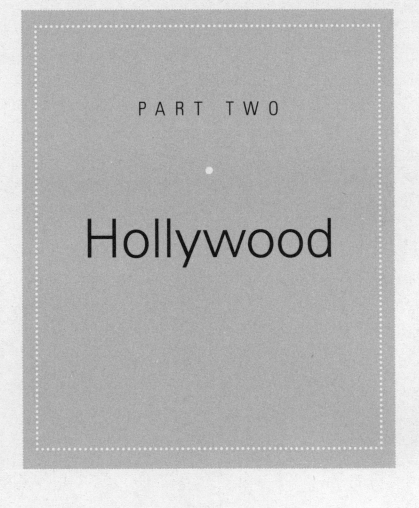

PART TWO

·

Hollywood

1

....

I'M A BIG believer that you should work at something you love, and also the reverse—love the work you do. But I'm also enough of a realist to know that's not always possible, and putting food on the table and paying for a roof over your head often takes precedence. Modeling provided my entry into acting, but I wouldn't have thought of it on my own. Credit goes to my mom, who came home from the mall one day having noticed the Esprit store was sponsoring a model search and suggested I try out.

Me, a model? Though people had come up to me every once in a while and said, "You should model," to me, real models were named Cindy Crawford, Claudia Schiffer, Linda Evangelista, and Paulina Porizkova. Denise Richards didn't exactly have that ring to it—not that I heard anyway. Nor did I have the figure; my boobs were tiny and my body was still more surfer girl than curvy young woman. But my mom said I should think in terms of having fun instead of worrying about becoming a supermodel, which was the kind of practical advice that I relied on and now dispense myself. In whatever I do, whether it's decorating, skiing, acting, or cooking, I prepare as best I can, try hard, but realize I'll find the level where I'm supposed to be. Not every flower in the garden blooms, if you get my drift. But that shouldn't stop you from planting the seeds. Maybe the most interesting part about my mom's recommending the contest to me is that we were going through a rough period then. During my junior and senior years of high school, we frequently butted heads. I had a steady boyfriend and pushed for more and more independence, while she attempted to calmly but firmly apply the brakes before her daughter veered out of control. Part of her plan included channeling my free time into activities, and if modeling turned into something where I received positive feedback, so much the better.

She knew more than I did, so I shrugged and said, "Why not?" A few modeling classes followed before the competition. They were a rip-off. I don't know what else to say. Fortunately, I didn't put too much stock in the competition, which was held at a mall in Whittier, a suburb east of Los Angeles. My mom and dad drove me there and found seats in the audience while I checked in, along with the other girls, inside the Esprit store. The best part were the clothes we were given. I really enjoyed having professionals apply makeup and do my hair. That part was my idea of heaven. The rest, which included several trips down the runway in different outfits, happened on its own, with little nervousness compared to the concentration I put forth to walk and smile as we'd been instructed. At the end, I came in second place, a pleasant surprise to me, though the real surprise came as I stood with my parents. A representative from an L.A.-based modeling agency introduced himself and said he wanted to represent me. I glanced at my mom, who was busy trading skeptical looks with my dad. Though this had been her idea, she didn't know whether the guy was legit and what I'd be getting into if we took the next step.

But we did. A short time later, my parents drove me to the company's Los Angeles office for a meeting. We saw the agency was legit and grew comfortable as we met and spoke with the other agents there. The representative explained the business was mostly print work, with magazines and newspapers, and that with my looks, I'd fall into the young-adult and teen category. He painted a realistic portrait, from the long commutes to L.A. from Oceanside to the disappointment of not getting jobs for reasons that were beyond my control, and he asked if I thought I could handle it. I said yes, I supposed so. It was still a lark to me, after all, and in the back of my head I was also thinking it paid a lot better than scooping ice cream.

As we returned home, we marveled at the HOLLYWOOD sign in the hills above the agency's office, the view of the coast, and how we were less than two years from living in Downers Grove, where such a situation would have been beyond our imaginations. It made me once again appreciate my parents' attitude. It was rubbing off on me.

After working with several photographers to put my book together, the agency submitted my photos, and I was hired for a *Teen* magazine shoot. It was done in one day in an L.A. studio, and it was easy. My dad drove me up and back to make sure everything was okay; my dad wasn't comfortable with me going alone with a strange photographer. More print jobs followed, including shoots for *Seventeen* magazine and L.A. Gear. All were teen-oriented. Other than confiding in a couple girlfriends and my boyfriend,

James (more on him later), who drove me to the jobs, I kept my new career a secret. Talking about it seemed like bragging, and that wasn't my style. Nor was drawing attention to myself.

When the ads came out over the summer, some of my classmates noticed and asked if that was me in the magazines. Otherwise it wasn't a big deal. By my senior year, though, everyone knew I was modeling, and they accepted it as something I did, the same way others surfed, played volleyball, or became cheerleaders. Other than enjoying the money I was able to put into my bank account, I didn't take modeling seriously and had no plans to make it a career until my geometry teacher threw me off the college track.

I was a pretty good student, but geometry gave me a hard time. Like so many things, you either got it or you struggled. I had a hard time understanding the concepts. I always thought it was developmental. No matter how diligently I studied, my brain didn't get it. One day the teacher called me to his desk and said I probably couldn't get into college if I didn't pass geometry, and it didn't look as if I was going to pass. The news upset me, but I quickly turned to Plan B—acting. Though I hadn't been in any high school productions, I'd continued taking drama after we moved to Oceanside, and I still loved it. Ever since I'd seen the movie *Grease* as a kid, I'd wanted to be an actor. Don't know what it was about that movie, but that's what happened. When I was growing up in Illinois, it never seemed possible. But now we were much closer to Hollywood. Modeling consumed more and more of my free hours after school and weekends with the drive back and forth to Los Angeles. Still, I liked the idea of trying to act professionally in the future, and even better, I'd read of numerous actors who went to Hollywood straight from high school, so college wasn't a requirement. (Okay, anyone reading this who's in high school, I highly recommend you go to college!)

Others didn't share my enthusiasm or confidence. As my friends finalized their applications and some heard about early admission, a classmate asked what I planned to do after graduation. I said I was going to model and move to L.A. to become an actress. I'll never forget her expression. She looked at me as if I was insane. "What's your backup plan?" she asked. "I don't have one," I said. "That's what I'm going to do."

I suppose I was part realist and part dreamer, an admirable outlook for an eighteen-year-old, if you ask me. In fact, I would advise people of any age to look at the future with one eye focused on what's practical and probable and the other eye on what might be possible if you take a few chances. Life is dull without hope—hope that life will contain opportunities for something new, whatever that may be. In my life, it turned out to be adventure.

On the day after my high school graduation, my agency sent me to Tokyo for two months, explaining that American girls did well there. I wanted to go, but I was scared shitless. Other than a family trip to Disney World and our move to California, my travel experience was limited to camping and ski trips and visits to my grandmother's in Wisconsin. My parents took me to the airport, and I held back a reservoir of tears as I hugged them good-bye. Once on the plane, I spent the fifteen hours of flying time talking myself into being braver.

I'll never forget the pit I had in my stomach when we landed. It was nighttime, and I made my way through the airport holding a piece of paper on which I'd written directions to the apartment the agency had booked for me. Somehow, I found the right bus and made it to the apartment. A rep from the agency met me in front of a three-story building, escorted me upstairs, unlocked the door, handed me the key, and left. He never asked if I needed anything. He just left me there, standing in this place on the other side of the world, in the dark.

It got worse when I turned on the lights. I saw hundreds of cockroaches run across the floor and the kitchen counters. They were in the drawers and cabinets, too. Scared and sick to my stomach, I grabbed the key and my purse and dashed out of the apartment. Once I was on the street, though, I didn't know which way to walk. Wanting to call my parents, I chose a direction and went in search of a pay phone. When I finally found one, I couldn't figure out how to use it.

Though it was late, I saw a few people on the street, including one man who looked American. He turned out to be Eastern European and didn't speak English, and I ended up back at my apartment, waiting for daylight, when I could find someone to help me.

In the morning, I met some of the other girls who lived in the building and found out they'd gone through similar experiences. As they predicted, in short order, meetings, shoots, and an odd familiarity with the Tokyo subway system replaced my fear and disorientation. Tokyo is a gorgeous, clean city. Cabdrivers wear white gloves. The agency sent us on multiple calls every day, and the jobs varied from simple studio setups to elaborate location shoots. In one, I rode a roller coaster over and over, until I was dizzy and nauseous; and for a poster, the photographer moussed my hair into spikes that stuck out in every direction and hung toys from them. Crazy stuff. Modeling for me was an exciting job with cool locations and the chance to meet creative and eccentric people, but I still wanted more. I also set boundaries. Lingerie modeling was the most lucrative of the jobs in Japan, but I refused any job that required me to pose in my bra and underwear, which infuriated the agency. I wasn't altogether uncomfortable with my body, but I didn't have a figure that allowed me to brim with self-confidence in all departments; and being photographed in my underwear bothered me. (Ironic that, years later, I actually posed completely naked. Go figure.) In Japan, at the time, they actually preferred the models to be small-busted for the lingerie ads, which is why they wanted me. That just goes to show you that the people you see in magazines, catalogs, movies, and on TV have issues even though they choose to be in front of the camera. Often those issues are what directors or photographers are looking to capture; other times you pray the problems don't show. The point is, there's always more going on than you see. In my case, the agency barraged me with angry calls and threatened to send me home if I didn't reconsider. They didn't follow through, probably because I worked steadily, but my steadfastness did not make ours an easy relationship. I remember calling home and my dad was pissed that they were trying to get me to pose in lingerie. He called my L.A. agent to see if this was a legit agency I was at, and my L.A. agent explained that it was and that lingerie was a huge moneymaker for their market. I wish that had been explained before I left L.A.

Other girls were much less inhibited when it came to posing in lingerie, or even less, though that was the least of what some of them did. When hanging out together, I saw them use drugs, alcohol, and casual sex to deal with the boredom and loneliness of being away from home. I was there to work, not party, so I didn't get dragged into that scene. I did get terribly sick one night toward the end of my two-month stay following a sushi dinner. I managed to show up at a job the next day, but I was in such pain that someone took me to the hospital, where I wanted to stay, and would've, had one of the owners of the agency not shown up, spoken with the doctors, and informed me that I had to be at work the next day or they were going to sue me.

Fighting pain and weakness, I got through the shoot and then finished up my stay with a stomachache, but I still showed up to my jobs. When I returned home, I weighed slightly more than ninety pounds. My parents were shocked and livid. A trip to the doctor revealed that I had a parasite from the bad sushi. (I haven't eaten raw fish since.) Only when I recovered some of my strength was it apparent that, despite losing weight, I'd returned home having gained a ton of self-confidence, as well as determination to continue modeling and try to make it as an actress, too.

2

....

NEXT, I MOVED into an apartment in West Los Angeles with a girl I knew from modeling jobs. A beautiful California blonde I'll call Stephanie had dropped out of the business and enrolled in college, but she helped me celebrate when I landed my first TV commercial (for Paul Mitchell hair products) and then a walk-on part in *Life Goes On*, my first TV credit. Though I only worked a day, I loved being on the set. I loved the camaraderie the cast had with each other, and it looked fun.

After I really caught the acting bug, I still modeled to pay my rent. One thing I noticed about my gorgeous roommate was she had fabulous fake breasts. She inspired me to get my boobs done (more on that later!).

I eventually moved out of my apartment when a popular modeling agency wanted to sign me in New York. I decided to go to New York and spend six months working and taking acting classes in between. I lived in an apartment with five other models. Yes, there were six of us in this tiny two-bedroom apartment. I felt that this was what a sorority must feel like, only completely dysfunctional.

Once in New York, I continued building my book, and I actually worked a lot despite my height—or lack of—at five feet six inches. It's also when I got my first taste of being criticized about my weight. At the agency, every week we had to get weighed and measured. They used a tape measure for our thighs and our waists, hips, arms, you name it. Because I was on the shorter side, they wanted me very thin. I was five feet six and weighed 110 pounds. One day, the owner of the agency had a talk with me and told me the agency wanted me to lose ten to fifteen pounds. I'm not joking. The agency hired me a trainer and put me on a strict diet; they wanted me to drop the weight, and fast. This is where a young model (I was nineteen) could get very messed up in the head about body image. I was embarrassed in front of the other models who lived with me at the tiny apartment. I was the only one who was asked to lose weight. Despite being fat in their minds, I still worked. But I ended up saying fuck it. I didn't want a career as a model anyway. So I left New York and headed back to L.A.

Unlike in modeling, where my size and physique would limit my potential, I knew acting was different. (Well, depending on which role you play.) Also, acting was something I was passionate about. The door to success was wide-open to anyone, of any size, shape, look, and talent, and I decided to commit myself to making it my career, or at least try to. I signed up for acting classes with a respected teacher who ran a studio in Hollywood. I moved into a house in West Hollywood with a gay friend who was ten years older than me, stable, and a phenomenal cook.

Soon I was seeing fellow acting student Patrick Muldoon, who was also attending USC. Before Pat, my only serious relationship had been my high school boyfriend, James, but that relationship had ended after I returned, nearly a year earlier, from Tokyo. Pat was different. More mature, focused, and extremely bright. He had his sights set on a serious career, and we spent hours after class, in groups, or just the two of us, talking over coffee about acting and the future. It was fun, and I got to know him well before we ever dated.

When he picked me up on our first date, I introduced him to my roommate and sensed some awkwardness. In the car, Pat asked if he was my boyfriend or some kind of sugar daddy, which was quite funny. Later, after Pat dropped me off, my roommate was waiting up to find out about the date. He was also quite smitten with Pat. Pat and I would date on and off for years before anything progressed too quickly.

My friend helped me get a fake ID so I could get into all the hip clubs. I used that ID to try to get a cocktailing job. I was still modeling at that point to pay the rent. Now truth be told I'm twenty and look about fifteen. I give the owner a lot of credit for not hiring me; he clearly knew I was not twenty-four (per my fake ID). Actually, I ran into that club owner a year ago, and he reminded me of our interview. I told him I had a lot of respect for him for not hiring an underage girl. A lot of sleazeballs would've, but not this guy. So, with no cocktail-waitress gigs, I continued modeling, which took me to Japan once again to make some quick cash, and then I had a few bookings in New York.

Once back in L.A., I rented a studio apartment in a sketchy area of Hollywood. What sold me was that the place had pink carpet. It also had fleas. But the carpet was pink, so who cared? One day, as I left for acting class, a police officer stopped me and asked if I had seen anyone with a baby. Seeing my confusion, he explained, "A baby was taken from the building." "Like kidnapped?" I asked. He nodded.

Whether or not it really happened, I assumed other shady if not downright dangerous stuff was going on there, and I called my dad to help me move my crap somewhere else. When my parents pulled up in my dad's truck, I got an earful from them. They hadn't seen my apartment, and they were angry that I would've moved there in the first place.

I found a studio apartment in a building with security in the Valley, though in talking with the manager, I encountered a problem: I couldn't afford it. Not by a long shot. Luckily, they had one low-income unit available, and I qualified. After settling in, I decided to get more serious with turning acting into a real job.

One thing I had to do: change agents. I needed a theatrical

agent. I had professional headshots taken and sent them to agencies. The Harry Gold agency was the first to respond, and after
my first meeting, they signed me to their children's division. I
was a little confused until they explained that being able to play
fourteen or fifteen years old made me even more attractive since
shows wouldn't have to bother with the regulations that protected child actors on the set. Plus, I wasn't expected to have a
long résumé.

I have so many fond memories of that time in my career.
Barely twenty, I was carefree, hungry, optimistic, eager, fairly
naïve, resilient, untainted, enthusiastic, and full of the thing that
makes each day better and brighter no matter if you have one
dollar or one million dollars—that's the belief that something
wonderful might happen. I went to class every week, checked
in with my agent daily, and auditioned as often as possible. I
worked extremely hard. I took care of my body, said no to drugs,
and made sure I prepared thoroughly. One rule I always obeyed:
on the night before an audition, I stayed home and studied. I
took the work seriously. I wanted to be good at my job. And I
wanted to keep paying my bills.

Always concerned, my dad warned me about the high percentage of Screen Actors Guild members who were unem-
ployed. I told him not to worry. I planned on being part of the
percentage who worked. I truly believed it was going to happen,
and I must've sounded pretty convincing because my sister took
a year off from college to try acting, too. We had a great time.
We moved into a two-bedroom apartment in the same complex
while she waitressed and took acting classes with me. However,

she was too shy, and she didn't enjoy life in L.A., both of which made her realize acting wasn't for her.

At the end of the year, she moved back home—and just in time. Without my mom's cooking, she shrank to about ninety pounds. But I'm grateful we had that time together. It was wonderful to share a dream, and even better to have her around as mine started to become a reality. In early 1991, after my first two auditions with my new agency, I got my first parts! I had one of the most amazing weeks of my life when I landed small parts on two popular TV series, *Saved by the Bell* and *Doogie Howser, M.D.* Both happened the same week, which was hard to believe. But I wasn't about to argue with that kind of good fortune. Then I got a part on *Married . . . with Children*. My role was too small for an actual name; I was simply called Girl #2. But again, so what? I was getting hired to do what I wanted, what I loved, and earning money at it.

In early 1992, after my twenty-first birthday, I worked on *Beverly Hills, 90210.* I played Jennie Garth's cousin in an episode where her mom got married. I didn't have much to do, but I was thrilled to be on a hot show, one I actually watched, and in the spirit of full disclosure, I was a little intimidated by all the young star power there. But something began to happen with me, actually within me, on that set, and it continued into my next jobs, *The Ben Stiller Show* and *Seinfeld.* It was a change of mind-set, a subtle yet real transformation that was essential if I wanted to genuinely morph from wanting to act to actually being an actress. This is true of everyone. No matter what you do, at some point, you must ask yourself if you belong; not only if you fit in, but if what you're doing feels right—in my case, it was being on the set and working with actors. For a long time, I was one of those actors in coffee shops and class, talking about being an actress and going on auditions. Then, when the opportunities arose, and I couldn't be just another pretty face among the countless pretty faces in Hollywood, I had to look inside myself and find out whether I had the stuff to be an actress, whether I could deliver on a set of professionals. On *The Ben Stiller Show* I ran down the beach in a bikini, and on my *Seinfeld* episode, which ran in 1993, I played the network president's daughter and had to play innocent while George (Jason Alexander) stared at my cleavage.

It was weird to sit there and do take after take of Jason staring at my boobs, but I understood that was the joke, and I just tried to block out how I really felt. The cast was hilarious, and it was a treat to watch them work. They worked extremely hard to make every scene and every line and nuance within the scene look natural and effortless—and, of course, funny. I was privileged to get to observe them up close.

I saw that in others who were at the top of their craft, including Denis Leary on *Loaded Weapon*, George Clooney on the TV series *Bodies of Evidence*, Matt LeBlanc in the movie *Lookin' Italian*, and Dean Cain in the series *Lois & Clark: The New Adventures of Superman*. For me, those days were as much about watching and learning as doing, in fact more so, though as the parts grew ever so slightly, I worked hard to make a good impression. I was on point, diligent, and prepared. I was always excited to share stories with my parents. Whether it was a movie or TV set, the process was slow and methodical, with lots of waiting around, chitchatting with new friends I made. Looking back, though, I see that those idle hours were almost more important than the work itself—in terms of observing how everyone from the cast to the crew did their jobs—so that I knew exactly what was expected of me when it was my turn in front of the camera. I was also making enough money as an actress to support myself. Barely, but I was still supporting myself. Looking back, I was so grateful. I remember learning that craft service was free food. After receiving a plate of snacks, I asked a PA, "Who do I pay for it?" I was shocked that there were just tables of free food all day for everyone.

I also loved the moment when I got my first cast chair on set with my NAME on it! It was for a pilot I did for Aaron Spelling. The whole cast was excited, and we all took pictures. That was cool. When you play Girl #2, you don't get that. I also remember the first time I had a job on location and production flew me first class. I had never flown first class in my life! (It's a SAG rule to fly actors first class—and a great rule at that, I might add!) Plus, when you travel they give you per diem to pay for your food and other expenses while away from home. On *Starship Troopers*, we called it "free money." Despite the good times, trust me, I don't forget those days when we weren't able to order room service or buy the latest designer jeans.

3

....

IN THE MIDST of that run, I moved into a house in West Holly-wood that I shared with another girl and two gay guys, one of whom was in my acting class. He was friendly with Chuck James, a boyish-looking junior agent with ICM, one of the industry's major theatrical agencies. Ambitious, Chuck was smart and self-confident, with sharp instincts, good taste, and an innate sense of the way Hollywood worked. As we got to know each other, he took an interest in my career, and while he wasn't in a position to sign me, he offered to represent me unofficially—or to "hip pocket" me, as it's called, meaning he'd serve as my agent without formal papers. It also meant leaving the Harry Gold agency, which was a risk. But my gut told me it was time for a change, so I went with Chuck.

We'd barely finished shaking hands before he got me the lead in *Tammy and the T-Rex*, a low-budget movie about a murdered high school student who reunites with his high school sweetheart, Tammy, after he's been turned into an animatronic tyrannosaurus. I played Tammy, Paul Walker played opposite me, which wasn't hard to take, and, yes, I knew the movie was cheesy. But it was a movie! And it was so much better than hearing my agent say, "They went with someone else." And, as Chuck reminded me, at this stage of my career it was important to work and build both a résumé and a reputation.

Reputation? As a new actress, I was cognizant of building relationships with two constituencies, the public and producers. Chuck was clear in his advice: I had to think both short and long term. Hollywood's internal hard drive is based on relationships. So in addition to talent and looks, I wanted to be known as someone who was well liked, easy to work with, and professional, and I tried on all accounts. It was important—especially a decade later when the shit hit the fan and I needed to rely on the goodwill I'd built. Hollywood is full of people with talent and looks. A good attitude went a long way. The little things my parents had taught me starting in childhood, such as a firm handshake, participating in conversations, and saying thank you, were even more important as an adult.

That was certainly true when I auditioned for Aaron Spelling, the most successful producer in TV history. He was producing a new series called *Pier 66*, and I was extremely nervous when I met him. In addition to being a legend, I knew he had the power to change my life. No pressure, right? But he put me at ease almost immediately with a pleasant, personable manner. As we talked, he made me so comfortable that I forgot whom I was speaking with, which was part of his gift. While I gabbed away, thrilled to be in conversation with the man who'd cast Farrah Fawcett in *Charlie's Angels* and Joan Collins in *Dynasty*, he studied me with the seasoned eyes of a sculptor, assessing whether I fit his vision, and I guess I did.

I got a callback, then tested for the pilot in front of the network, negotiated my contract in case I was approved, which was damn exciting to think about what I might get paid if the show went, and then, finally, to my amazement, I got the part. I was beyond thrilled. Fittings started immediately, and Mr. Spelling was at every appointment, offering opinions or quietly nodding his approval as he puffed on his pipe. His hands-on involvement made a lasting impression on me, and I'd think about him again years later when I did my reality show, and later still, when I lent my name to hair products and perfume. If it had my name on it, I had to be involved in as many decisions as possible.

After the fittings, the cast flew to Fort Lauderdale, Florida, where we planned to start shooting the series if ABC picked it up, which was expected. Why wouldn't they green-light an Aaron Spelling show? The man was a TV genius. All the talk among the actors was about having to relocate to Florida while we were in production. I didn't mind. It wasn't a bad place to live. As we waited for news, my sister called with wonderful news of her own: She was pregnant! I screamed. I was going to be an aunt. My parents weren't thrilled with the circumstances; my sister didn't plan on marrying the father, and my parents weren't fans of his—kind of a double whammy of disappointment. On the other hand, they were excited about becoming grandparents and loving up a little baby.

It was actually the start of a difficult but satisfying time for all of them. After giving birth to a son, Alec—named after Alec Baldwin, whom both of us liked—Michelle lived for the next five years with my parents. My dad had left the phone company and, with my mom, opened a coffee shop called Jitters. Michelle ran it until she met her husband, Brandon. (They would get married a month after Charlie and I, and have two boys together. So it turned out great.)

In the meantime, ABC didn't pick up the series.

At that point, however, I had no choice but to go back to auditioning and plugging away. I came close again when I scored a good-size role in *P.C.H.*, a *Melrose Place*–type pilot about five coeds at a college near the ocean. With Jack Scalia, Sally Kellerman, and Casper Van Dien in the cast, I sensed it was going all the way, but at the last minute the network changed its mind and turned it into a made-for-TV movie. People asked how I dealt with the ups and downs, and the truth is, I didn't. I'd spend weeks feeling excited and full of hope at the prospect of working on a weekly show and making good money, and then a single phone call would erase everything but the dream.

And it didn't get any easier on my next job, *919 Fifth Avenue*, a glitzy, sexy nighttime soap spun from bestselling author Dominick Dunne, starring Barry Bostwick and Lisa Eilbacher. Mine was a small but crucial role of a girl who was raped and murdered early in the second act, which meant I cried and screamed rather intensely in a short amount of time, then died. At the table read, I recited my lines without the histrionics that would be part of my actual performance, while making sure to add, "Of course, I'll be crying and emotional here."

After I finished, though, one of the producers appeared at my side. I could see he was angry, but I couldn't figure out why. Asking to speak to me privately, he motioned to the corner.

"Why are you screwing around here?" he asked.

"What are you talking about?" I replied.

"Why aren't you crying? You didn't cry at the table. The part calls for you to cry. Are you prepared? This is not a joke."

Confused, I began to tremble. "I'm sorry. I've never been to a table read where someone actually cried and screamed."

"Well, now you have. The network wants us to fire you."

"What?"

"The network wants to do a read with you right now," he said.

"What? I have to read again?"

"They want you to reaudition. Right now."

"Why?"

"Because you fucked up," he said. "They have no idea what you can do. And frankly, neither do I."

Suffice it to say, his comments and crass delivery destroyed me, yet I had to hold it together, at least on the outside, which was a feat of acting itself. At the same time, I was livid with this producer and all of the other producers at the table for not sticking up for me. They could've told the network exec who'd complained that they had my crying on tape. They knew I could cry. But they caved, and I felt ambushed. I ran into a dressing room and called Chuck. I told him what had happened and said I wanted to leave.

Though sympathetic, he said I wasn't in a position where I could walk out and piss off a network, and he was absolutely right. I knew better, too. You don't walk away because something doesn't go your way. You figure out a solution. In my case, it meant going back to the table and doing it the way everyone wanted, full out. Believe me, when the network execs and producers reconvened to reaudition me, I had no problem crying. I cried so hard one of my contact lenses popped out. They kept me in the pilot.

A month later, I was working on an episode of *One West Waikiki*, the Glen Larson–produced drama with Cheryl Ladd as the world's best-looking medical examiner, when the *919 Fifth Avenue* producer called—the same one who'd ripped me. Now he said if the pilot was picked up, they were going to reshoot my part with someone else and add me as a series regular. I was stunned. "The network loves you," he said.

In the end, *919 Fifth Avenue* didn't go to series. But I remember hanging up from that call and then turning to my mom and sister, who were with me in Hawaii for a girls' week of pampering, and telling them the news. "It was that asshole producer who made me cry," I said. "Now he says they want me as a regular." My mom, my sister, and I traded high fives. It didn't make sense, but not everything does at the moment it happens, such as my parents' move to California, my decision to become an actress, or the producer's tantrum when I didn't cry at the table read. Often the only way you ever know for sure if you made the right move is to fix the problems that are fixable, don't worry about those out of your control, and keep marching forward.

My philosophy in life has always been, if it's meant to be, it will be. Things happen for a reason. One door shuts, another opens. If I didn't get a part, a better one was waiting for me. I'm not saying I never got disappointed or broke down in tears, but, in general, I saw the glass as always half-full.

PART THREE

·

Getting Naked

1

....

WHAT DOES IT mean to get naked?

Over the years I would ask that question many times and for different reasons, and come up with a variety of answers, though the first time I posed that question it meant just that: What does it mean to get naked? I had read Joe Eszterhas's script *Showgirls* and was on my way to audition for director Paul Verhoeven. The two of them were responsible for the huge box-office success of the sexy thriller *Basic Instinct*, and the hype around *Showgirls* made it the hottest property in Hollywood—and also one of the scariest. The story about a young girl who climbed the Las Vegas ladder from stripper to showgirl required near-constant toplessness and seemed likely to push the boundaries of an NC-17 rating.

After reading the script, though, I knew the nudity was very real. This was a movie where whomever was cast as Nomi would have to step fully into the role and out of herself, and I wondered if I could do that. At twenty-four years old, I wasn't far from those days in Japan when I refused to pose for pictures in a bra and underwear, and this movie required exposing way more than that. I had to ask myself if I could do it, and if I answered yes, what would it mean to get naked? Would the risk be worth it? Would I be cheapening myself?

From the many discussions I had with Chuck, I knew one thing for sure: people in and out of the business were going to talk about whoever got the role. It was going to be impossible not to have an opinion, and whatever that opinion was, it was going to be extreme. As written, the role was one of the most daring parts for a young actress in years, if for no other reason than what she was going to have to show, physically *and* emotionally. It was definitely a dance on the high wire without a safety net. Despite being comfortable with my body, I was not exactly the exhibitionist type. But after reading the script several times, I was able to talk myself into a place where I could see the nudity was about the character, not me. Once I got there, I decided to go for it; I was ready for the high wire.

As I did with every audition, I tried to dress appropriately for the role. For this, I wore a simple dress. It let the director see my body without being overt.

He also saw a lot of other actresses and eventually opted for Elizabeth Berkley, the talented and beautiful actress from *Saved by the Bell*, who was also looking to make the leap from TV to movie star. In the end, reviewers savaged both the movie and Elizabeth, the latter unfairly, and I suppose I was lucky, in a way, to have not gotten the part. But I've always admired Elizabeth's courage. I remember reading an interview in which she said that, like the character, she was turned on by challenge, and that's why she sought the role and went for broke. I understood. I would've done the same thing. Interestingly, at least from my vantage, she was much more exposed in the aftermath, when she was hurt and having to put on a brave face in the wake of terrible criticism, than she was in any scene in the movie. But all of us are the same way after any project, whether you've made a movie or given a PowerPoint presentation at the office. Everyone has boobs and a rear end. But when your emotions are raw and on the surface, you're naked in a whole other way that feels even more vulnerable.

So what does it mean to get naked?

I remember feeling way too exposed in another way when I worked on the TV movie *In the Blink of an Eye*. It was a month-long shoot in Utah, and rather than put me up in a hotel there, the production company had me fly back and forth to Salt Lake from L.A. I probably would've been fine with that if not for an extremely turbulent flight from Hawaii a year earlier that had turned me into one of those fear-of-flying freaks. (I'm a much better flier these days.)

On my first trip to Salt Lake, I landed covered neck to ankle in red, swollen, itchy hives. A friend from the movie met me at the airport and took me straight to the emergency room. They gave me a shot of adrenaline and I looked more normal than not by the time I got to the set. I wished the same thing had happened on my next trip into town. I flew in at night and went straight to my hotel, with my hives, hoping they would be gone by morning. The PA called at 5:00 a.m. to say he was in the lobby to pick me up. I lied and told him that I ate something that I was allergic to and had a horrible reaction. I had to lie, I didn't want him to think I was nuts. When he saw me, he said, "Oh, wow, yeah that's pretty bad!" My lips looked like a collagen experiment. My whole face was blown up! I was so embarrassed! He took me to the hospital where I told the doctor the truth and he gave me a shot of adrenaline. He gave me that plus a Benadryl, so I was zonked by noon and barely able to get through my scenes. The point? If you take your shirt off, people stare once or twice. But if you have mysterious red things on your lip and it's puffy for no apparent reason, people stare all day long, thinking, "What's going on with her?" And though I didn't know it then, it's much worse when you're in the grocery store and your face is on the cover of every tabloid and gossip website. But in many other situations I've bared my soul and been far more exposed than if I'd bared my body. The same is true for all of us.

So what does it mean to get naked?

It depends.

2

I HAD TO broach the subject again on the movie *Starship Troopers*. It was about a year and a half later when I auditioned for the role of starship pilot Carmen Ibanez, and Paul Verhoeven, the director, remembered having met me. The big-budget film was based on Robert Heinlein's Hugo Prize–winning novel about a time in the future when people had to battle giant bugs threatening to destroy human life. I auditioned five or six times before they had me screen-test with Casper Van Dien, who was cast as the lead, Johnny Rico. Since Casper and I had auditioned so many times together before our screen test, we had good chemistry and hoped that would come across. We were hoping we both would be cast in the movie. This process went on for a couple of months. A few days after our screen test, I met Chuck at his office before going to a premiere with him, and he was grinning like a kid with good news when I walked in. I'd gotten the part. I was so excited to get that part. It was a lot of auditions and hard work, and I couldn't believe I actually got a movie that was going to be in a theater! The first person I called was my mom. She was crying, I will never forget it. She was so happy for me! A few of my actor friends were like, "It's a six-month shoot?! Ugh!" But I didn't care that the shoot was long, I was working on a real studio movie.

In Hollywood terms, this was a major step up. I was going from guest spots on TV shows to a key role in a more than $100 million budget motion picture that was going to open around the world. Before shooting began, I did a four-episode arc on *Melrose Place.* An actor on the show and a couple of the production people couldn't believe I was leaving for "the bug movie," as they called it. But I was excited. I was going to be flying supersonic planes and shooting weapons—all pretend, of course, but very cool. Also, when Paul turned his attention to casting my character's romantic interest, I suggested my friend Pat, who'd made a name for himself on *Days of Our Lives* and *Melrose Place*, and he got the part, which made it like a party.

All of us became good friends: Casper, Pat, Jake Busey, and Dina Meyer. We all were at the same stage in our careers— basically thrilled to have the job, which didn't seem like work anyway. To get us in the kind of shape where we looked like "fearless and square-jawed" fighters, as *Entertainment Weekly* described us, we worked out daily with a trainer at the studio gym, and then, after about a month, they sent us to boot camp in Wyoming, where we had to tough it out in rough conditions, including a freak blizzard that caught us unprepared. Everyone's sense of humor came out and we had a bonding experience as we huddled together in a tent in the middle of the night to keep warm.

Work on the movie itself was long, hard, and deeply satisfying, especially when Paul said he was satisfied with a scene. His approach each day was intensely passionate and creative, and all about executing his vision. One afternoon, he asked to speak with me. We sat down and he said he'd written an additional scene into the script, a love scene, and it required me to take my top off. He asked how I felt about that; if I was willing to do it. The multiple nuances contained in that question made it incredibly hard to answer on the spot. I'm also the kind of person who has a gut reaction to something, but I've taught myself to then step back for a moment or two (or three) and think about it from different angles to make sure my first instinct is correct. I consider the immediate effect of my answer, the longer-term effects, and then the best- and worst-case scenarios. In this instance, my radar was flashing a red warning light. We were well into shooting. Why did the director suddenly want me to add this sexy scene? Was it needed in the movie? Did it relate to my character? Or was it going to be one of those scenes where the action paused while the young actress showed her breasts? Cue the teenage boys in the audience. Beyond that, I had to consider the man asking. He wielded a measure of power in the business; what if I said no? What would the repercussions be?

To his credit, when Paul asked, he did it with no strings attached. He truly left it up to me, and after careful consideration

I said no. I didn't think it related to my character or the movie, which had more than enough going on between the action and the undercurrents of social and political commentary. Though he tried to persuade me otherwise, Paul didn't try so hard that I felt pressured, and ultimately I didn't do it. Thankfully, I never experienced any fallout.

In a way, that movie spoiled me forever. My agent, Chuck, told me not to get used to it. My next movie could be a gritty independent with a crappy budget. The sets on *Starship* were incredible. Delicious food was catered every day. My sister felt as if she'd entered a different world when she visited the set with her two-year-old son, Alec; I took my parents to the red-carpet premiere in Beverly Hills; I received positive mentions in reviews; and after its opening weekend, November 7, 1997, *Starship* was number one at the box office. I knew I'd taken a step forward in the business. This was fun. I wanted to keep going.

I couldn't wait to see what was next.

3

....

FOUR MONTHS AFTER wrapping *Starship Troopers*, I received the script for *Wild Things*, which I recognized for what it was—a smartly written erotic thriller set among high school students highlighted by a threesome designed to turn on every red-blooded moviegoer between the ages of fifteen and fifty. Neve Campbell had already been cast in the lead role, along with

Kevin Bacon and Bill Murray in crucial supporting parts. They were still looking for the other females, the spark that would ignite the fire, so to speak.

I've never had a problem with sexy movies. *Basic Instinct* and *9½ Weeks* are examples of excellent adult-themed movies that also cause your inner thermometer to rise. Liking them is one thing, but starring in one is another. I read *Wild Things* several times, thought about the nudity, and talked to Chuck about the pluses and minuses of taking on such a role, before I finally agreed to audition.

Director John McNaughton liked me, but I still auditioned five times without hearing anything other than they liked me. I read on tape, and then I had to read with Neve. While I was waiting to hear if I got the part, John went into the editing room with Paul Verhoeven as he worked on *Starship* (the movie hadn't come out yet) and watched several scenes. After my auditions, my reading with Neve, John's watching scenes and asking Paul how I was to work with, I got the call that I got the part! After I was cast, they cast Matt Dillon. What a fantastic group of actors for me to work with on my second movie in a theater!

I was so excited. I thought it could be a really good movie and the character was opposite my character in *Starship.* But it required me to cross lines that I knew I would one day have to cross for the right part. I just didn't think that decision would be now. I always said if it was the right project and I felt that it was right, then I would do it. So here it was. While Neve had a no-nudity clause in her contract, I was still the up-and-comer without any leverage, and my breasts might as well have had their own billing separate from me. Storyboards with sketches of them went back and forth between my agent, my lawyer, the director, producers, and the studio. They were the subjects of conference calls and memos, including how much of my nipple could show. It was strangely bizarre. Mostly, I was mortified.

After many back-and-forth negotiations, it was agreed that only one of my breasts would be filmed, though the reality was they shot both, knowing I wasn't going to sue, and they were right. After the breast storyboards, the producers asked if I was okay French-kissing Neve on camera. Usually it's that pretend movie kiss, but they wanted a kiss kiss. I thought, "Okay, I'm sure she has nice lips." And she did. On the set, though, I found an ally in Theresa Russell, who played my mom in the movie. An awesome presence on- and offscreen, she sat down next to me one day and advised me "to be a bitch if necessary." In other words, if I felt that I was being taken advantage of, I could say no—and, according to her, should not hesitate to say it whenever my inner alarm went off.

"Really?" I said. "I can?"

"You have to," she said. "You need to take care of yourself." Right after I was cast, I had my breast surgery (more on that later) and had three weeks before I left for location—Miami.

We shot for twelve weeks in Miami. I'd flown there on the same flight as Neve, who was lovely and like me in that she was focused on the work. As soon as we got to Miami, we did a table reading (the dreaded table read; I was well prepared). We had fittings, tanning (*Wild Things* is where I discovered self-tanner and have been hooked ever since), and every week they set up nail appointments, which I loved. I was tan, manicured, and in good shape. They also set me up with a trainer and I had cheer-leading lessons. It actually felt like camp. I think we were there two weeks before we filmed. I met the rest of the actors when I got to Miami. I was so intimidated to go from *Starship Troopers*, where nobody was famous, to a famous cast on this one. I was the only unknown out of all of us. I have to say, they all made me feel comfortable. Especially Kevin Bacon; he was in-credibly supportive. We had group dinners and rehearsal before we started shooting. By the time we filmed, all of us had a lovely camaraderie. My second studio movie and I was spoiled again, with a fabulous trailer, amazing catering, and a huge per diem for living expenses. I had a blast working in South Beach. My sister even came out to visit a few times.

In the movie I played a popular cheerleader from a wealthy family who cries rape after her advances on a young high school counselor (Matt's character) are rebuffed. His life and career in the small town fall apart despite his denials, and then things get worse when Neve's character, a bad girl from the poor side of town, lodges a similar charge. But at the trial, Neve admits to lying, a multimillion-dollar settlement is negotiated, and just when it appears the problems are solved, it's revealed that the three of them have planned the scam together. As a skeptical de-tective played by Kevin Bacon begins to reassess the outcome, the three key players meet up in a cheap hotel outside of town and celebrate their new wealth with a threesome.

We filmed the threesome toward the end of the shoot. As we approached the threesome, my anxiety grew worse. The first time we were scheduled to shoot it, I got to set nervous. I went through hair and makeup and body makeup. I was just finishing getting some bronze makeup on my tush when the AD came to my trailer to tell us the director was sick and couldn't film our scenes. I was so relieved! I honestly think he may have been more nervous than the actors. I'm sure it's hard for a director to shoot those kinds of scenes, too. They have no idea how an actress is going to react when the moment comes for disrobing. I've heard stories of actresses backing out at the last minute, and I'm sure John had heard those stories, too.

When the time came to shoot it for real about a week after this, I got anxious again. Looking back, being a new, young actress, I think I had a lot of guts to do this part. It was very sexual and risqué. It could've gone in a negative direction for me. Since I got the part, and many girls auditioned for it, I figured if I didn't take my top off, someone else would've. Aside from the nudity, this was a cool character for me to play. I was lucky to have such a juicy role; it was actually almost two characters. That's what I focused on when it came time to shoot the risqué scenes. *Focus on the character and block everything else out.* I had the threesome and a scene with just Neve and me in a pool. The day of the shoot I began to feel vulnerable, and when I looked around for support, I realized it was one of those situations I'd have to face alone, like when I was a kid and jumped off a high dive for the first time.

John shot the scene in small segments, and the crew was reduced to the minimum, though, despite a closed set, a small army of people still watched on monitors and other places we couldn't see. The action was discussed beforehand and carefully choreographed. It began with Matt and me. Then Neve arrived. I was undressed, Neve and I kissed, and after all of us climbed on the bed, Neve poured champagne on my naked chest. It was steamy, for sure. However, of the two most revealing scenes for me—one where Matt raises my skirt and removes my underwear and the other when my top comes off—I was much more concerned about how my butt was going to look.

Ridiculous, right? But I didn't want my ass to look huge, and in the privacy of my trailer I practiced posing in front of the mirror with my makeup artist until we came up with an incredibly awkward way of curving my back to create what we thought was the perfect angle for my tush. It may seem hard to believe, but as we did the scene, and I stood there while Matt lifted my skirt, I was picturing the image I'd seen in my trailer and thinking, God, I hope the cameraman is getting the right shot. I guess it worked. After the movie opened, people asked if that was really *my* butt. Yes, it really was; to get it to look that way I was standing like a jackass. And Neve and I really did kiss—twice. Once during the threesome scene, and a second time when the two of us were alone in a swimming pool, having a fight that turned into a passionate seduction. Though the action was planned, it was still a bit surreal to get in a pool with Neve at four in the morning, kiss, and remove each other's tops, and it turned out both of us were fraught with nerves. John was on edge, too. In fact, at his suggestion, Neve and I went into her trailer and shared a pitcher of margaritas before we did the scene. Neither of us had ever kissed another girl. We shrugged, clinked glasses, and went for it on-screen. Everyone has a first time.

4

....

THE MOVIE WAS red-hot before it opened. The buzz was incredible. Photos of Neve and me locking lips were leaked. *Entertainment Weekly* put Neve, Matt, Kevin, and me on their Spring Preview cover. After the premiere, I told reporters, "All I wanted to do was cringe during those scenes while everyone was watching." I prohibited my parents from attending the premiere. They saw it on their own, but my mom said my dad walked out during the naughty parts. (I gave them a heads-up when they were coming.) Paul Verhoeven was actually the first person to call me after the movie opened. He was so supportive and teased me about getting naked in that movie, but not, his. He said he would find me a sexy movie for us to do together. (Come to think of it, I'm still waiting for that movie, Paul!)

With *Starship*, I did press with the junkets, premiere, and a couple appearances and a Planet Hollywood event in New York. With *Wild Things*, I did a ton of press, including *The Tonight Show*, newspaper and magazine interviews, and a promotional tour. Racy photos lifted from *Wild Things* exploded across the Internet. The result? All of a sudden, I found myself, at age *twenty-six*, recast in the public mind as Hollywood's newest sex symbol. It was my first taste of the way the media can shape or reshape reality, creating an image that is virtually independent of the truth, and while not unpleasant, it was both strange and surreal. What would people expect of me? Was I really this person? If not, who was I? And most important, who did I want to be?

On the plus side, I had a blast showing up at events such as the MTV Movie Awards, where Neve and I lost out on the year's Best Kiss to Gwyneth Paltrow and Joseph Fiennes for *Shakespeare in Love*. I also traveled to Italy, where a designer made an original gown for each celebrity. It was my first trip to Europe. I took my boyfriend, Pat, and the trip was magical.

We flew to Milan, where I was fitted for my gorgeous gown. Then we were driven to Florence for an event. On the first night, we were invited to someone's villa for a pre-event dinner, where I ate something that didn't sit well, and I spent the night doing everything I could to not throw up. Poor Pat. At 2:00 a.m., he was walking the streets, looking for Imodium, while I was sprawled on the cold balcony floor praying I'd feel better. Fortunately, it was just a twenty-four-hour bug. The next night, after losing about three pounds, I put on my gown and we went to a palace for the most incredible party. Before returning to normal life, we spent a few more days in Florence, visited Pat's grandfather in Croatia, and wrapped up the trip with a spectacular time in Venice.

Amid all the hoopla and attention, I could see how people got in trouble when they began believing their press. After being in a couple of hit movies, everyone was nice to me. Invitations to parties and premieres came in. *Playboy* magazine asked if I'd do a pictorial. It was like going to high school one day and being accepted into the popular group, except that I knew I wasn't any different from before. Thank goodness my gut always told me to take things slow and be wary of things that seemed too good to be true.

Having the press was lovely, but I didn't want to be just the flavor of the month.

I had two studio movies in theaters that people actually went to see and I wanted to continue working. To this day: with every part I've had, I always think I'm going to get fired, and after every job, I always think I'm never going to work again. I am always focused on what's next.

I was amused at finding myself called a sex symbol. Sure, it was a wonderful compliment, but the reality was, at twenty-six, I had my good days and bad days, like anyone else. I still remembered being called Fish Lips and Bucky Beaver. It was all about keeping perspective. Hollywood's glamorous perks were fabulous, but I'd been raised to know that if I wanted to feel beautiful and sexy, it had to be because of how I felt on the inside, not from anything I could buy or wear.

I know, cliché. We hear that over and over, but only because it's true. But here's something I learned early on. First of all, I am a girly girl and I love having my hair done or makeup put on by a professional. I just do. Expert stylists do it so much better than I do. To this day, I still can't do my own hair well, and I have tried. Makeup—I have learned good lessons from some of the best, but I still like having it done. I would be lying if I said I didn't. I love the fabulous clothes I get to wear on a photo shoot or at an event, as well as the cool wardrobe created for a character and beautiful diamonds borrowed to go with a couture gown. But none of that stuff lasts. Even the most expensive designer clothes are only worn for a few hours at most, and at the end of a red carpet event, the jewelry gets returned and the limo drives away. Then you're back in your sweats or T-shirt eating ice cream at the end of the night watching TiVo. I can't remember all the times I felt like Cinderella at the ball. Even those women who've been attending big events for thirty years will tell you the trick is feeling great about yourself when you're out of your golden carriage and back in your pumpkin.

It doesn't matter who sees you naked; you have to feel comfortable in your own skin, and believe me, it took lessons to learn that and time for me to feel comfortable in my own skin. When I did get all dolled up by professionals and saw an image of myself on a magazine cover, at times I felt unattractive when I didn't look like that image I was portraying. I had to realize that is the image portrayed on that magazine cover and I don't have to look like that when I get gas in my car.

After completing press for *Wild Things*, I made the movie *Tail Lights Fade* in Vancouver, and when I got back to L.A., I was greeted with the news that I'd been offered a role in the film *Drop Dead Gorgeous*, a satire of beauty pageants already boasting Kirsten Dunst, Brittany Murphy, Kirstie Alley, and Ellen Barkin. Talk about every struggling actress's fantasy. Instead of having to audition, this plum role had been offered to me, I didn't have to audition for it!

The movie shot over the summer in Minnesota, and I took my mom, who'd grown up in that area of the country. She enjoyed revisiting that area and hanging out with the girls. Kirsten and I got manicures every week together, and all of us went out at night for dinner. I especially loved Kirstie, and to this day we are still friends. *Drop Dead Gorgeous* has a scene with me singing about Jesus and dancing with him. While we were shooting that scene, extras were in the audience. I guess a lot of them were religious, and not having read the script, they walked out in the middle of filming. They were quite offended by my flinging Jesus around during my silly dance.

When I returned home from Minnesota, I was enjoying the rest of the summer with friends, and Pat and I were hanging out. Again, thinking I was never going to work again, I was reading scripts and anxiously wanting my next job. I was happy making money, and my accountant thought it was time to think about buying my own home. I was thrilled! At heart, I am a nester, a nester who loves to travel, obviously influenced by growing up in a strong, stable family with parents who were do-it-yourselfers and constantly redoing or tinkering to make a home cozier and more comfy. I wanted that, too.

I made a dream list—a list of dreams—something I think everyone should do starting in their twenties, and then go from there. Start ticking them off. The quality of your life is different when you pursue your dreams rather than put them off. It had taken my dad a few years to redo our house in Downers Grove. He did a little bit every day. But he finished. Then it was on to California. Acting had been on my list. So had taking my mom to Hawaii. Now a house with a big enough yard for a dog topped it. I started house hunting but was fearful. What if I bought the damn house and wasn't able to pay my mortgage?

5

IN THE FALL of 1998, I auditioned for the part of Dr. Christmas Jones, "the next Bond girl," in the movie *The World Is Not*

Enough. Though I'd never seen a James Bond movie (I know that's hard to believe), I knew being a Bond girl had its pluses and minuses. Some women never escaped the stigma, others used it to their advantage.

On a good run, I asked Chuck whether that was the right move for me, and after some debate, I auditioned. A short time later, they flew me to London for a screen test. I went in late November with my dad, and the two of us spent Thanksgiving going over my scenes for my screen test. I did fittings one day at Pinewood Studios, a screen test there another day, and then my dad and I crammed in a day of sightseeing before returning home.

The following week a reporter from *Details* magazine was interviewing me for a cover story when Chuck called with exciting news. I got the part. I didn't understand the full magnitude of being the next Bond girl until I turned on CNN a few nights later and saw myself on the screen, the subject of a story announcing that I'd been cast as nuclear weapons expert Dr. Christmas Jones opposite Pierce Brosnan in the next James Bond movie. And it wasn't just on CNN. It was everywhere—other TV entertainment shows, magazines, and newspapers here in the United States and around the world.

News broke the first week of December 1998 and production began in January 1999. I flew back to London with my mom for wardrobe fittings and to find an apartment that would be my home for the next six months. We found a cute two-bedroom in a building near Kensington Palace. It was adjacent to Hyde Park, which was beautiful even in the middle of January. For the first two weeks, I loved being there; then I started to feel lonesome and homesick. I always loved being on location for a movie. I love bonding with the cast and hanging out, getting to know one another. This experience was different. I had nobody to hang out with. Pierce was with his family, the crew all had families in London, and Sophie Marceau was in and out to Paris, where her family lived. I was lonely on this long shoot, but it was a huge opportunity and I sucked it up, focused on my work, and asked my mom to fly out and see me. My first scene was with Dame Judi Dench. I literally felt sick my first day. I had one line and it kept me up all night. I never sleep the night before my first day on a new set. It's like your first day of school. I was up all night with anxiety of my one line with the fabulous Judi Dench.

It was a Bond movie. Everything was over-the-top, starting with the plot, which had James Bond saving the world from a nuclear meltdown. Luckily the folks behind the scenes were laid-back, starting with Pierce, who was in his third go-round as the international spy. Bond movies are hugely successful, and the producers making these movies have a well-oiled machine. Many units are going at once. When I wasn't at one, I was doing stunts at another. Not as much was required of me—I was fine running around in shorts and a tank top (like every top female nuclear scientist). I returned to L.A. when I had some days off to do press and photo shoots for *Drop Dead Gorgeous*. I also got a makeup campaign for Max Factor, I flew ten hours and went right to my photo shoot. I looked crappy after getting straight off the plane to shoot a makeup ad, but thank God for hair, makeup, and fabulous lighting. When I found myself with still more time off that spring, Pat flew out and we spent three days in Paris, where I discovered what it means to be in the public eye.

As we explored the city, which I loved, I noticed people were staring at me. Not just glancing the way you do when you think you recognize someone; they were checking me out. At first I thought it was my imagination, but whether Pat and I were in a café, walking along the river, or strolling in and out of Left Bank shops, I saw people looking at me. It made me a little self-conscious. What the hell were they looking at?

Then, one afternoon, we walked into the Virgin Megastore and Pat and I saw enormous posters of Neve and me from *Wild Things* on the walls. It had been retitled *Sex Crimes.* Oh my God, I was *that* girl and it was called *Sex Crimes,* which for some reason embarrassed me a little bit. Afterward, I started noticing the poster all around the city—in stores, subways, everywhere, and people started coming up asking for my autograph and a picture with me. I still get shy when people ask me to take a picture. I always think people walking by are looking at me taking a photo with someone and going, "Who the hell is that?" Same with the paparazzi, I feel so stupid when there are quite a few of them snapping away and people wondering who the heck I am. But that was a tiny prelude to the scrutiny that came my way.

When *The World Is Not Enough* opened in November 1999, my life became all about promoting the movie. I attended nearly thirty premieres around the world, starting in L.A., though the month before that was filled with meetings, fittings, photoshoots, and preparation for interviews. I did a huge spread for *Vanity Fair.* Annie Leibovitz shot every Bond girl. What a shoot that was! I was thrilled to be doing my first world tour for a movie. I had a blast. I went to so many different countries. The hair and makeup artist who did all my press shoots, whom I had become good friends with, came with me. We had fun! We flew to Ireland for our first stop, and Pierce and I presented an MTV award to Britney Spears. After the awards show, we all went to a private after-party where Bono and Iggy Pop performed. It was an unforgettable night. From there we went to the London premiere of Bond, and then it was Belgium, Berlin, Paris, Madrid, Finland, and Amsterdam. I saw so many beautiful places and met the most incredible people. That to me was the biggest gift I got from doing the movie. I was so blessed to travel and see the world and it was a whirlwind. As soon as we landed in each country I went straight into hair and makeup, pulled a dress out of my trunk that was packed by a stylist, did a press conference, press junket, premiere, party, bed, and off to the next place in the morning. Unfortunately, the reviews I got made it hard to suck it up during my interviews. Except for Roger Ebert, reviewers followed the harsh route of the *Chicago Tribune*'s Michael Wilmington, who wrote, "There's the script—and that's the problem." Actually, most were meaner, and I felt I was unduly singled out. "How could she play a scientist in hot pants and a halter top?" critics asked. The barbs were so bad that Michael Apted told *Entertainment Weekly*, "I hope I didn't hang her out to dry."

I knew you had to have thick skin in this business, but this was my first time receiving criticism, and it stung. It was so public. Talk about being stripped naked. Right before going on MTV's *Total Request Live* before heading to Europe, I found a *USA Today* review of the movie in the dressing room. I'd been taught to avoid reviews for this very reason. This one slammed the movie, and me! How was I going to go out on live TV and put on a happy face about the movie? How the hell was I going to do nearly four weeks of press across Europe knowing people thought the movie sucked and I was a terrible actress? Devastated, I called home. Both of my parents got on the phone and provided the support and common sense I needed to move forward.

"It's only other people's opinions, it's just a review," my dad said. "It's not who you are."

"Denise," my mom said, "just hold your head up high. Let people see the real you. They'll know the difference. You have a lot of fun ahead of you."

She was right. But I was depressed about it. I had a horrible pit in my stomach and I was embarrassed doing my interviews, feeling as if every journalist were making fun of my performance. Whether or not it was true, it was how I felt. For the record, years later *EW* named me the worst Bond girl, so I was right. Some were making fun of my performance, but, hey, I was a Bond girl! The European tour more than compensated for the criticism. Before the London premiere, the producers gave Sophie and me each a lavish thank-you gift—a diamond and sapphire bracelet. Later, I gave it to my mom. My business had lots of perks, but none came close to the gift of being able to go home to my family. There were probably some movies I shouldn't have done along the way that weren't best for my career, but they did allow me to buy a home for my parents and I bought a new truck for my dad's fiftieth birthday; it meant a lot that I was able to do that for my family.

·

PART FOUR

Good Time Charlie

1

....

AFTER FILMING *BOND*, I bought a Tuscan-style house in the
Pacific Palisades and a dog (I couldn't wait to own a home with a
yard to finally get a dog), a Boston terrier that I named Lucy, so
when I came back from Europe I returned to my house. It was
an incredible feeling to unlock the door and walk into my home,
then wake up the next morning next to the beach, pad around in
my T-shirt and pajama bottoms, make coffee, and think about
building my life. I wanted to get married and start a family. As
Pat and I had gone our separate ways, I did not let being single
stop me from going after the things I wanted. I decorated my
house and continued working. I filmed *Undercover Brother*
(on location in Toronto), *Empire* with John Leguizamo in New
York, and a few other projects, and I brought Lucy along. I went
out with friends and stayed busy. My life felt full. Sure, at times,
I wished I had a special someone with whom I could curl up at
night and talk about the day or plan my tomorrows, but I didn't
stress about it, relying on friends to keep me from feeling lonely,
and keeping the faith that I'd find the right guy. I believed my
soul mate was out there and that fate would lead us to each other
when the time was right.

A part of me enjoyed the freedom of being single. I didn't

have to worry about answering to anyone other than me. I lived in the moment, and loved it. I didn't want to be with someone just to be with him. It had to be right, even if it was "right" for only a short time. It had to feel good.

Soon that status changed—and so did everything else, forever—when I accepted a four-episode arc on the hit ABC series *Spin City* and renewed my acquaintance with that show's star Charlie Sheen. We'd worked together the previous summer on the movie *Good Advice*, a romantic comedy about an investment banker who loses everything only to discover what's really important in life. After I took the movie, Charlie called to talk about the project, and we ended up on the phone for two hours, discussing it and a thousand other topics, most of which had nothing to do with the movie. I was still with Pat at the time and wasn't romantically interested in Charlie. But we had chemistry right away, and I thought this would be a fun project and he'd be cool to work with.

When I showed up on the *Spin City* set, we hugged and spent a few minutes catching up. I reminded him that when I last saw him on the movie, he'd just signed on to replace Michael J. Fox on *Spin City*, and I'd predicted he'd do an awesome job. "And guess what?" I told him. "I was right."

My guest stint as campaign strategist Jennifer Duncan was part of a larger casting stunt for sweeps that also saw Michael return to the show, along with additional guest stars Farrah Fawcett, Queen Latifah, and Olivia d'Abo. I shot two episodes back-to-back, and Charlie and I flirted the whole time. The chemistry was undeniable. As we said good-bye at the end of the second episode, Charlie suggested we get together outside the show. When I said that would be nice, he promised to call, and a couple days later, he did.

We arranged dinner, but then the day before our date, Charlie called to tell me the World Series was on. He was an obsessive baseball fan and was in a bit of a dilemma. He wanted to go out to dinner, but didn't want to miss watching the game.

I understood. I didn't want him to miss the game either. From working with Charlie on the movie and two episodes of *Spin City*, I knew he was a little superstitious, and I would've felt terrible if he missed an important game because he was out with me. He may have taken it as a sign or something, and as I told him, it wasn't a big deal to me. I really did understand.

"You're telling the truth?" he asked.

"Yes," I said. "We can go out to dinner another time. Don't worry about it."

Charlie was silent. I could hear the wheels spinning in his head. He asked if I'd consider watching the game with him at his condo, and he promised to take me out to dinner another night. I said sure, why not? I didn't see a downside. I saw two fun oc-casions. Only my dad didn't think it was a good idea for me to go to Charlie's house. He advised me to wait until I knew him better. In my dad's eyes I was still his little girl, and he worried about me. I didn't listen to him.

Indeed, dinner out became dinner in. Instead of the sexy dress that I planned to wear to the restaurant, I threw on a pair of jeans and a cute top and went to Charlie's swanky bachelor pad to watch the game with him. He greeted me warmly; he was relaxed and showed me a spot on the sofa in front of the big-screen TV. As much as I like a fancy night on the town, it was actually nice to be at his place—just the two of us, getting to know each other privately.

And Charlie and I did just that. Rather than order in food—looking back, this is kind of ridiculous and very L.A.—I brought over the plastic-wrapped, portion-controlled meal I had delivered to my house, and he heated up a portion-controlled meal of his own from a similar delivery service. I picked up our favorite flavors of Häagen-Dazs, chocolate for Charlie and mint chip for me. I know—low-cal meals and ice cream? Unlike most guys I've been around during a game, he kept the volume low enough for us to talk, which I liked. Afterward, we watched a movie that his mom had recommended, and when I got up to leave, we had an awkward little moment by the door. I thought, is he going to kiss me? Do I make a move first? Do we not kiss at all? When he hesitated, I thought, screw it. I'll be bold and make the first move—and so I planted one on him.

It was spectacular. Definitely butterflies. Then I went home. By the way, the game was great! And his team won!

Few things are as exciting as meeting someone you like. Life is just that much better. It pushes the boring stuff into the background and fills every moment with excitement, especially the beginning. The newness is just wonderful. You think about a million different things, all involving that new person. Well, at least I do. No matter the time of year, every day smells fresh and springlike, ripe with possibilities: nothing is as intoxicating as love. A few days later, he kept to his word and took me out on a dinner date. I got my makeup on and did my hair. A friend came over to help me pick out something to wear. That was fun. We decided I should look cute, but sexy, without trying to look sexy. We came up with black Theory pants and a sexy top with Jimmy Choo heels. If only he knew how many outfits I tried on before he got to my place.

Oh, another thing that impressed me: Charlie picked me up! I know it's a small favor, but it doesn't happen as often as you'd think because L.A. is so spread out. Ordinarily, when you live thirty or forty minutes from each other, as Charlie and I did, you meet at the restaurant or a guy will send a car to pick you up. Given that Charlie had a bit of a schlep, I thought he was quite the gentleman to pick me up (now, having been married to him, knowing he hated to drive, this was a big deal). My dad was also impressed.

He took me to the restaurant at the Hotel Bel-Air, one of my favorites. It's secluded and stunning. We strolled through the lush gardens, across a bridge where we stopped to look at the swans nesting beside the pond. Even at night, it was gorgeous and romantic, as was the restaurant, where we were seated at a corner table. Conversation with Charlie was effortless and I enjoyed talking to him. Aside from his being incredibly handsome and sexy, I loved his openness. He was confident without being cocky, and self-deprecating. Believe it or not, I also saw an endearingly shy, sensitive part of Charlie.

He made no attempt to avoid his issues with his three years of sobriety, which had been, as he noted, chronicled in the press. I had no experience with addiction, and in hindsight I was quite ignorant about it, but I admired his strength in getting sober, his determination to stay sober, and the effort he made to work on himself. Getting through all of that and being so humble about it impressed me.

As dinner progressed, I liked Charlie more and more. People have said that I'm attracted to so-called "bad boys," and I've done a lot of thinking on that subject. In fact, I have gotten defensive in the past. The truth is, I don't like "bad boys." I like calm and stability. I grew up in that kind of stable and traditional home, with that kind of father. My dad was home for dinner at six every night. When it comes to men, I'm attracted to a guy who has lived and enjoys life, someone who is strong. He's not surprised or overwhelmed by life; he appreciates the good times and digs in when the going gets tough, and he doesn't run when difficult issues come up. Doesn't that sound better than a "bad boy"?

Okay, confession: during our dinner I had a premonition that I was going to end up with Charlie. It was surreal. We were on our first real date, but to me it seemed like the start of a lifetime (shit, little did I know). I honestly pictured him as my husband. I can't explain it further. I'd never had such a strong and clear premonition. It made me feel good. My mom always said, you'll know when you know. After dinner, we strolled around the hotel grounds and shared a passionate kiss in front of the beautiful swans. It was a prelude to a wonderful, romantic night back at his condo.

When I left the next morning, I was a teeny bit embarrassed to walk through Charlie's lobby while wearing his T-shirt and carrying my high heels in my hand, but I knew it probably wasn't the first time the security guards had seen a woman leaving Charlie's place like that. And, hey, if every girl left with a shirt of his, he probably wouldn't have had any left! I knew I was special.

2

....

AFTER OUR ROMANTIC rendezvous, it was time for me to return to *Spin City* and finish my remaining two episodes. Charlie and I decided to keep our new relationship under the radar. Let's play it cool, we told each other. We were just friendly costars. But then there was reality. When I got to work, a magnificent arrangement of roses was waiting for me in my dressing room. The card read, "Welcome Back," and it was signed, "Mr. Green," Charlie's alias at the time. After breathing in the sweet scent, I walked into makeup with a big smile on my face. As I said, I loved that feeling of my heart opening up to someone new and being full of anticipation of what was going to happen next. I was happy to be there again.

Even though Charlie and I tried to play it cool on the set and keep our interactions appearing professional, I'm sure the cast and crew knew something was going on. We were emitting sparks whether we liked it or not; plus, during lunch, I snuck into his dressing room—and snuck out looking disheveled.

C'est la vie.

After my episodes were finished, Charlie and I continued our romance. Though we weren't "out" publicly as a couple, we moved forward at high speed. I met his parents, Martin and

Janet, who couldn't have been nicer, his brothers and his sister, and also his then-sixteen-year-old daughter, Cassandra. My parents lived two hours away, and we hadn't yet had time to make the drive down the coast to see them. Then, one morning, Ryan Seacrest interviewed Charlie for his morning radio show on KIIS FM, and he asked the usual personal questions, specifically, "Are you dating anyone?" Instead of skating around it, though, as is normal practice, Charlie said, yes, he was. Ryan asked who, and Charlie said, "Denise Richards." It may sound like high school, but we hadn't talked about our dating and keeping it quiet. Given people's obsession with celebrity relationships, it was something we needed to discuss. Or maybe we didn't need to. Maybe it was best that it happened just like the relationship itself, spontaneously. After the interview, Charlie called and told me that he'd "outed" us as a couple on the air and hoped I wasn't upset. I was taken aback by it, but, really, I was pleasantly surprised and happy that he was confident enough early in our relationship to do that. "No, I'm not upset," I said. "I think it's great."

We ate Thanksgiving dinner with our respective families and then met up later that night at his place. The next day we flew to Hawaii, our first trip together. You can tell a lot about a person when you travel with someone, especially whether you're compatible. Charlie and I traveled well together. During the trip he gave me a present, a little blue box that was unmistakably Tiffany. I couldn't believe it. Inside, was a heart-shaped diamond necklace. I was speechless—and touched that he didn't just get me a beautiful gift, he actually went to the jewelry store and picked it out. He put thought into it, and that's what meant so much.

Later, we went to a luau at the hotel, and a personable young couple who explained they were newlyweds asked if they could take a picture with us. We said sure, and lo and behold, a few weeks later, those pictures showed up in *Us* magazine. The couple had removed themselves from the photo. It was really uncool, but we shrugged it off. You can't go around not trusting people.

We returned more in love than ever, and we decided to take a drive down for Charlie to meet my mom and dad. It took about two and a half hours to get to their house from L.A. We loaded Charlie's Mercedes with my four dogs and headed down. I noticed he was a bit quiet on the drive and seemed nervous. He kind of made a joke that he didn't meet too many girls' parents. I reassured him that my mom and dad would love him, but he still seemed nervous.

An hour into the drive, his car locked up and stopped right in the middle of the freeway, and he had a panic attack. I thought, shit, I have all these dogs in the car, we're going to get rear-ended on the freeway, and he is panicked. The excursion was not going well. Before Charlie's superstitious mind convinced him that this was a sign from God that he wasn't meant to meet my parents, I switched places with him, got the car unlocked, and took off down the freeway again.

There was a charm to Charlie's nervousness. He may not have thought so, but I did. Likewise, when he finally met my mom and dad. I can't speak for how Charlie felt, but he looked at ease, and they did, too. They liked him immediately. People have often asked if his past concerned me, or if it concerned my parents (if it did, they didn't say anything to me at the time), and the truth is, no, my parents were great about it, and so was I. As far as I'm concerned, the past is what it is—the past. You can only judge a person by their actions in the present, and the man I met didn't show any signs of the past.

3

....

RIGHT BEFORE CHRISTMAS, I got a phone call at 5:30 a.m. It was Charlie. He'd been nominated for a Best Actor in a Comedy Golden Globe for *Spin City*. It meant a lot to him, and he was genuinely excited for everything it meant. It was validation of all his hard work professionally and personally. I couldn't have been happier for him. I felt blessed to share it with him.

Right after Christmas, Charlie and I left on a romantic winter holiday getaway to the Miraval spa in Tucson, Arizona. Going to this spa for a week of pampering was a dream vacation. Oprah had been to the Miraval spa. And I was thrilled to have met a man who loved the idea of massages, facials, herbal wraps, and healthy foods as much as I did. What woman's heart wouldn't melt when her man asked, "Are you going to try the body scrub and a seaweed wrap?" After we arrived, and a few minutes later, as we checked into our room, unpacked, and slipped into our pajamas, I noticed Charlie seemed distracted, and I wasn't sure what was going on.

A moment later, I found out. Charlie had something special on his mind. "I can't wait until New Year's," he said as he got down on one knee in front of me and asked if I'd marry him. At the same time, he opened a box and handed it to me. Inside was a gorgeous 4.5-carat, round diamond ring. I'd never imagined getting proposed to by someone wearing boxers and a T-shirt while I was in a tank top and pajama bottoms, but I swear to God, I couldn't picture a more romantic moment. Of course, I said yes!

"I was going to wait until midnight on New Year's," he said. "But I couldn't do it. I couldn't hold out."

"I'm glad you didn't," I said.

I woke up the next morning and called my parents with the news. Surprised, they offered enthusiastic and what I took as genuine congratulations. Despite the whirlwind courtship, my parents never questioned our getting married so quickly. I'm sure they had conversations with each other privately. But they knew me well; I was an adult, and when I made up my mind, that was it.

Over the next week, as the rest of the world learned about our engagement, I enjoyed this new chapter in my life. I constantly held my hand in the sun and looked at my diamond sparkle. I loved my ring. I loved what it meant. I was a fiancée. I couldn't wait to be married to Charlie. I felt unbelievably fortunate to have met him at this time in his life. As he told me, in battling his problems he'd evolved into a healthy, open, and humble person. His career had taken off again. He had confidence. And now he was in love. Life was working out for him, as he'd been told it would if he got himself together. I felt similarly about myself. I'd turned thirty and knew I'd found the man with whom I wanted to build the rest of my life. As touched as I was when Charlie shared his dreams and made me a key part of them, I was equally gratified at how easily he fit into my dreams. Our compatibility seemed to underscore my belief that fate truly did connect soul mates when the time was right. You just had to be patient and ready.

In January, we attended the Golden Globe Awards. I found a classic gown by Giorgio Armani and got my hair and makeup done at Charlie's condo. It was fun getting ready together and sharing this moment that meant so much to Charlie. It was also the beginning of our moments as a couple; in our first public outing, we proudly walked the red carpet at the Beverly Hilton, holding hands, posing for photos, and answering questions from dozens of reporters. Yes, we were engaged. Yes, we were in love. Yes, things were great. Charlie's father and sister went with us to the Globes. Martin, who was also nominated in the drama category for *West Wing*, exuded proud father when he looked at his son.

Inside the ballroom, Martin sat with the *West Wing* cast and Charlie and I took our seats at the *Spin City* table. Ironically, given events that would take place in the future, I sat between Charlie and Bon Jovi guitarist Richie Sambora, who was married to Charlie's costar Heather Locklear. It was my first time meeting Richie, and that's all that happened. We said hello and not much else that evening. I was head over heels in love with Charlie, who won that night and told the world in his acceptance speech that he loved me, too. It was a magical moment.

To the press, our relationship was a great story. Charlie was the comeback kid, and with me on his arm and a diamond ring on my finger, it looked like the classic case of the good girl reforming the bad boy. Except that wasn't the case. I didn't have to reform Charlie. He was already reformed. As I said, his past was his past and I wasn't judging him for it. I believe our experiences make us who we are, and Charlie's past appeared to have made him a wiser and better man. He was in a good place, and he was grateful to have been given a second chance at life.

Following the Golden Globes, life was sublime. We alternated nights between his place and my place in the Palisades. In our free time, we watched movies, sports, and had dinner at our favorite Italian restaurant near the beach. We had the best times just sitting in bed and eating ice cream and talking all night. When I'd turned thirty in February and a girlfriend gave me those flowers with that card that said the best times were ahead of me, I nodded in agreement. It seemed they were, starting with our wedding.

Charlie and I were in sync on that, too. Both of us wanted an intimate wedding for family and close friends. We didn't want it to be huge. We wanted it to feel more like a fun, elegant dinner party where we'd be able to talk to each guest. We decided eighty guests was the perfect number.

Once we picked a date, we decided to hire a wedding planner to coordinate the arrangements. I interviewed a handful of planners and picked my favorite, Mindy Weiss, who then met Charlie. He approved, too. Mindy, who became a close friend, had done the most spectacular parties and weddings. She was easy to talk to, a great listener, calm and sweet, she thought outside the box, and she seemed unflappable. She clued straight into us when I explained the most important part of our wedding was the food. Charlie and I wanted great food. Mindy had some suggestions for a caterer, but we wanted our favorite restaurant, Giorgio Baldi, to make the meal. Unfortunately, they didn't cater events. Mindy stepped in, and I don't know what she said, but they changed their mind, and not only were we thrilled, we knew Mindy was perfect to steer us into our wedding day.

Even though there are some things I don't agree with in the Church, I still wanted to have a Catholic ceremony. Martin introduced us to a friend of his, Father Michael Kennedy. According to Catholic tradition, we took pre-cana classes, which I loved. Taking them privately, we filled out a questionnaire about our beliefs and goals, and our methods for handling conflict, and the process made me feel even closer and more deeply connected to Charlie. We were also happy Father Kennedy agreed to marry us outdoors instead of in an actual church and told us it would still be recognized by the Church; at the time, it meant a lot to me to have a Catholic ceremony. As for my wedding dress, several designers offered to make it. That kind of generosity was beyond my imagination. But I had my heart set on wearing one particular designer, Giorgio Armani, and he wasn't among those who'd offered. Nevertheless, I asked my publicist if she could ask if Armani would be interested in making my dress. I knew it was a long shot. I mean, who gets her wedding dress designed by Giorgio Armani?

I did! Not only did Giorgio Armani say he would design my wedding dress, he also wanted to make dresses for my maid of honor (my sister, Michelle), my mother, as well as tuxedos for Charlie, his best man (his closest friend, Tony Todd), and my father. I was blown away. I'd expected him to politely say thanks but no thanks, but instead this was way more than I would've dared to dream. However, there was a condition: Mr. Armani also wanted us to fly to Italy and meet his design team and asked if we would attend his fashion show as well. Some condition!

Of course, I said yes, and then I called Charlie. He was excited for me and knew for a girl that it was the ultimate fairy tale.

3

....

AT THE END of March, after Charlie wrapped *Spin City*, we got on a plane for Italy. This really was a fairy tale for me—flying to Italy to meet Giorgio Armani and have him design the most special wedding dress a girl could ever hope for. Once there, we met Mr. Armani at a villa where his design team was waiting for us. Again, fantasy time! Mr. Armani was stunningly handsome in person, and a gentleman. He couldn't have been any nicer. He didn't speak much English, but through his translator, he mentioned that since we didn't want Charlie to see my dress, they were splitting us up. Then the fantasy really took off. The men's team ushered Charlie into one part of the villa, and I followed Mr. Armani and the women's design team into another room, where they showed me numerous sketches they'd already done and then tons of fabrics they'd pulled for me to look at.

I was honored how hard they had been working on my dress. We narrowed the sketches down to a dress that was more form-fitting and simple instead of a full skirt at the bottom. They suggested a beaded, long-sleeved, lace jacket to wear over the dress for the ceremony, and then I'd remove it during the reception. We also went with a veil that was quite long, almost a train. I listened, nodded, looked, and tried to picture it all put together, and at first I thought it might be too much for our smallish wedding. However, once I saw everything, I knew it was absolutely perfect. During my fitting, a gentleman brought me a note from Charlie saying he was thinking about me. I didn't think the day, already surreal, could get any better, and yet it did.

After our fitting, Mr. Armani invited us to his personal villa for lunch, and Casa Armani, as you would expect, was exquisite. It was perfect. Charlie and I felt like the Beverly Hillbillies. We traded nervous glances through the meal, fearful we might break or spill something. But we had an amazing time, enjoying good food and conversation together. The meal couldn't have been better. The art was museum quality. Even the air had a unique fragrance. It was the quintessential once-in-a-lifetime experience.

The next day Charlie and I attended Mr. Armani's fashion show, and in keeping with the theme of the trip, we were dressed head to toe in Armani, which had been sent to our hotel. It was Charlie's first fashion show, and he was excited, and cute. Right before the show, Sophia Loren was ushered in. She stopped to say hello to Charlie, who had met her through his father many years earlier. I was in awe. Meeting her, the most beautiful woman in Italy, was the icing on the cake.

We were lucky to spend a few days in Paris, where Charlie had an event at Disneyland Paris. The two of us ran around the theme park like a couple of kids. I still have a picture of us on a roller coaster; Charlie's face is priceless, and to this day our daughters love that photo. Once back in L.A., the vibe changed slightly when we got the news that *Spin City* had been canceled. We knew the realities of the TV business: ratings were everything, and *Spin City* had struggled to keep viewers. But we were surprised. Charlie took it hard. I couldn't believe it. Only two months earlier he'd won a Golden Globe. We hugged and talked, and I was glad I could be there for him, offering support and comfort. Hopefully that took some of the sting out of disappointments such as this one. I knew he'd be there to help me if the situation were reversed. We had each other now. We were a team. We'd figure things out. Charlie was talented, and I knew more work would come his way. We were getting married in three months. We had a wedding to plan. We had our lives to live together.

I didn't think three months was much time to plan a wedding, but if anyone could pull it off, Mindy could, and indeed she had everything under control. Anytime I worried about something, she calmed me down. Mark's Garden created gorgeous flower arrangements for the tables, with lots of red roses and some champagne grapes, and since I love gardenias, he suggested a large gardenia in front of each guest's place setting, which was just the kind of little touch I loved. Our favorite part was picking out the wedding cake; a large box of samples was delivered to our home, and we picked through the different flavors. Mindy helped us with the seating, and that left just one detail—our first dance.

Neither of us danced, and the idea of a solo in front of our families and friends made us wish we could find stand-ins. But that wasn't an option. We decided to take private dance lessons. Since we had no confidence in our abilities, we hired the best teacher we would think of, famed choreographer Debbie Allen. She was great, and learning with Charlie was new and fun and lots of laughs. I found myself looking forward to our lessons.

"See, I told you," said Debbie, who put together a romantic routine for us.

One night, Charlie came home and said he had a surprise for me, but he wanted me to guess. He wouldn't give me any hints other than to say he'd seen an old friend. He was smiling ear to ear. I couldn't figure out what kind of surprise he meant. Then I saw his wrist was bandaged. "You didn't!" I said. He nodded, his grin growing even bigger. "Yup."

I knew instantly. He'd gotten a tattoo. I couldn't believe it, if only because he was getting three lasered off. He removed the bandage and there it was, my name, freshly inked and shining in the light like baby skin. I let out a big "awwww." I think a tattoo can be sexy, certainly intimate, and meaningful, and Charlie's was all three. No one had ever gotten a tattoo for me. I jokingly said he should've kept the tattoo on his ankle, the letter *D*, with a pair of angel wings, which he'd gotten for his first wife. As I told him, he got lucky marrying two girls in a row with the same first initial.

Well, being that I didn't have any ink on my body and had never planned on it, I quickly decided to follow his lead. I was going to get a tattoo (perhaps I should've followed my gut; it's the kiss of death to get someone's name imprinted on your skin, trust me). At the time, I thought, how could I not after his grand show of affection? I eventually did get a tattoo, but I waited until after we were married. I had other matters on my calendar—such as my final fitting for my wedding dress. Mr. Armani's team flew out to L.A., and my mom came with me to this one. I'll never forget her face seeing me in a wedding dress for the first time. She stared at me from across the room, smiling, as her eyes filled with tears, and then suddenly she was crying. "I'm just happy," she said. I'm sure I'll do the same when my girls get ready to walk down the aisle.

I was ready when the big day finally arrived. The night before our rehearsal, the press learned the wedding was going to be in the lush backyard of *Spin City* creator Gary David Goldberg's Brentwood home, and in a last-minute change of plans we staged the rehearsal in our condo's banquet room. Everyone piled in and we went through the motions as best we could, sharing nervous laughs about having to be there because of paparazzi. Father Michael had both families sit in a circle and asked each person to say something they were grateful for and then offer us a wish for the long journey that would be our marriage. Hearing all those loving thoughts turned me into a sniveling sap. It was beyond sweet. Then all of us retreated to a fabulous dinner at the Hotel Bel-Air, the place Charlie and I had our first date, and finally, late that night, Charlie and I went our separate ways. I wanted the next time he saw me to be when I walked down the aisle.

I woke up the next day feeling rested and full of anticipation, yet determined to enjoy every moment, and I did, especially spending it with my mom and sister. I went over to Gary's house early, bringing a gift for Charlie—a watch engraved on the back with our wedding date and the words "Time stood still." Once he arrived, my dad took it to him. We got ready in separate rooms. I don't know where the time went; it certainly didn't stand still. Though the day was spent getting ready with my mom and sister, I had no idea where the hours went when I finally got in my dress and heard the music playing outside. Peeking outside, I took deep breaths and felt my heart thump excitedly in my chest.

Everything felt good and perfect, as I'd hoped. I couldn't have been happier. Neither, it seemed, could my parents, whose mix of excitement, jitters, and unabashed love for me was adorable. I gave my mom a kiss and then held my dad's hand until it was time for us to walk down the aisle. At that point, I went into some kind of parallel universe where I simply counted my steps, smiled, made eye contact with Charlie, who looked dashingly handsome, and thought, "Oh my God, I'm getting married."

Charlie and I exchanged vows under a magnificent old tree festooned with more than two thousand red roses that appeared to the eighty guests as if they were floating in the nighttime sky. I'll never forget the intoxicating smell of the roses combined with candles everywhere.

Indeed, when I took a moment to survey the scene, it looked gorgeous and magical, like the fantasy I'd envisioned, and I couldn't have felt any more beautiful than I did in my antique-satin gown and high-heeled Manolo Blahniks. It was all perfect: the string quartet, my bouquet of white and ivory roses, the snippets from our love letters that Father Kennedy read during the ceremony, and finally our parents lighting a candle for us. We created a wonderfully romantic day, and we shared it with the most important people in our lives. We were able to indulge, but you don't need a lot of money to accomplish the same thing. It's the spirit that matters and provides the memories. After we kissed, I surprised Charlie. A gospel choir filed in wearing black baseball caps embroidered with the initials CD and sang "Take Me Out to the Ball Game." He loved it, and it got everyone in a party mood. As our guests filed in to the reception, Charlie and I snuck off by ourselves to have a moment to soak it all in. We were married. It felt surreal and wonderful. I loved him so much and was honored to be his wife.

The rest of the night was pure fun. Our first dance, to Journey's "Open Arms," was special, and I have a beautiful picture of Charlie kissing my hand and dipping me. We fed each other cake; I tossed my garter, and guess who caught my bouquet? Charlie's teenage daughter! Later that night, Charlie and I checked into the Beverly Hills Hotel. He carried me through the door. Our limo driver captured the moment with one of those inexpensive throwaway cameras. While cheap, it did the job and caught a special moment on film.

After spending two days in the hotel, we flew to Anguilla for a picture-perfect honeymoon of sun, sand, and sightseeing. One day, we took a boat ride, and when Charlie introduced me to the captain as "my wife, Denise," I melted. I loved the way that sounded. I couldn't believe how drastically my life had changed in the eight months since our first good-night kiss. It kept getting better and better, like the best dream ever.

4

....

ONE OF THE first things I did as a newlywed was to change my last name to Sheen. I decided to use my maiden name only for work. I also sold my house, gave all my furniture to my parents, and moved into Charlie's house. I'd stayed there countless times before, but something was different, permanent, and hilarious when I pulled into the driveway with all my clothes. I turned to my four dogs in the back and said, "Well, we're home."

Even though everything in the house was done in black, from the marble floors to the carpet to the kitchen, I made the transition easily. Charlie thought it would bother me to live in a home that had the look and feel of a busy bachelor pad, but other than wishing for a little more warmth, I was fine. As I repeatedly told people who asked that question, including my husband, the past was the past. I'm someone who's able to start fresh, whether it's moving on after a disagreement or moving into a new home. It's healthier.

I did encounter some strange features, such as the bedroom door that was bulletproof. A fire pole was in the closet (which one of our cats fell through, but he was okay) in case a quick escape to the ground floor was necessary. And the house had a panic room. But with the right attitude, I saw these as perks. Hey, I'd never felt safer when I slept. The home itself, though, was great, and we could stay there in plenty of comfort until we saved up enough money to move. I know hearing me say that we had to save might sound strange. But we were like anyone else. We had to watch our pennies and put money in the bank if we wanted to move into a home that would be ours.

I'd heard and read and been warned that the first year of marriage is the most difficult. I also talked to my mom about the issues she and my dad had when they were starting out, at ages seventeen and twenty-one, with a baby, and compared to them, I counted my blessings. But the truth was, Charlie's and my first year of marriage was the best and easiest and the only good year.

I thought, "Well, if this is the toughest it's going to get, marriage is going to be a piece of cake." I was naïve.

But couplehood did seem to suit us. That year, I worked on a few different projects, including a small part in Richard Curtis's charming romantic comedy *Love Actually*, and Charlie took meetings for new projects. After a few of them, he zeroed in on one specific TV series, a new CBS sitcom called *Two and a Half Men*. One day he handed me a script and asked for my opinion. I curled up in a chair, started to read, and an hour later declared it a no-brainer. "This is a gem," I said. "You have to do it."

Charlie agreed and shot the pilot, which I thought turned out exceptional in every way, from the writing to the on-screen chemistry Charlie had with his costar Jon Cryer. The network thought so, too. Just before CBS's midsummer announcement that the show would be on their fall lineup, Charlie went to work on *Scary Movie 3* in Vancouver. In June, he returned home for our one-year anniversary, and we celebrated with a romantic three-day retreat to the Montage hotel in Laguna. A few weeks later, I visited him in Vancouver. The next day after our reunion I woke up with a surreal yet strong premonition that our romance the night before had left me feeling something I'd never experienced.

That's right. I had a sense that I was pregnant. Since I'd never been pregnant before, I had no idea what it would feel like, or if at this early moment, it would feel like anything at all. Nevertheless, I felt *something*, not physically, just a gut feeling. But I shrugged it off and went about my business, which is indicative of my personality. I told myself it probably wasn't anything other than my imagination.

After Charlie finished the movie, we squeezed in a getaway to Turks and Caicos. Pining for some relaxing alone-time before he started production on *Two and a Half Men*, which we knew at the outset would require long hours, we spoiled ourselves with spa treatments and workouts. I got massages, took yoga classes, and did Pilates, though instead of feeling rested and invigorated, I felt the opposite, queasy and light-headed. I wanted to blame it on the heat, but a little voice in my head said, "It's not the heat"

I ended up opening my laptop, searched "early pregnancy," and read the symptoms.

Bingo.

I had every symptom except puking. Thank God!

I didn't tell Charlie yet, but when we got back home, I called my sister and asked her to send me a pregnancy test. If I went to the store and bought one, it would end up on the front page of *Us* magazine. When the test arrived, I took it in the bathroom, and waited. Within a few moments, I saw an extremely faint line, indicating positive. However, since the line was barely visible, I didn't believe it. Too impatient to wait for my sister to mail me another one, I hurried to the pharmacy and bought ten tests. Yes, I bought ten. I peed on all of them, too. And guess what? I saw the same damn faint line in every single one.

Why was it so faint?

Why not one way or the other? Why did it have to be wishy-washy? I wasn't a wishy-washy person. I was a one-way-or-the-other person.

Frustrated and anxious for clarity, I called the 800 number on the back of the box and explained the situation to the woman who answered. Without pausing to think about possibilities, she said it was positive—even if the line was faint. A line was a line, and that meant I was pregnant.

"Even if I can barely see it?" I asked.

"Yes, even if you can barely see it," she said.

"It can't be negative? How can it be positive if it's barely there?"

"Ma'am, even if it's barely there, it's positive."

I still wasn't convinced. After hanging up, I thought, what does she know? I needed a second opinion—I took the pee tests, lined those fuckers up, and I called in Charlie, who saw the pee tests set up across the bathroom counter and funnily enough didn't think I was nuts for having so many of them. Like me, he held each one up to the light as I filled him in on my conversation with the woman from the 800 number. Then he turned to me and nodded. The next day, my doctor ran a blood test and confirmed what the 800 lady and Charlie had already acknowledged. I was pregnant.

It was great news, but completely unexpected, and it took me a bit to get over the shock. I left the doctor's office and went straight to an audition. In fact I had to hurry there, so I wouldn't be late, which was typical of my tendency to overbook myself when I should probably be canceling appointments. But I was in such a daze from the news that I still can't recall what I auditioned for. My head was up my ass and, needless to say, I didn't get the part.

But sitting in traffic gave me time to actually process that I was pregnant, and I'll tell you what, I got excited—and not just because I would soon be able to drive in the car-pool lane. I believe things happen for a reason, and even though we didn't set out to have a baby at this time, it was obviously meant to be, and I was thrilled. I was suddenly part of something much bigger than myself. I believe children pick their parents, and I was so happy that this unborn soul was choosing Charlie and me. I was also surprised at how easily I got pregnant. I guess it's true what they say—it can happen the very first time!

And how did Charlie feel about becoming a daddy again? Of the two of us, I was the more spontaneous, the one who didn't always plan every hour of the day, the one who could roll with the punches. Charlie balanced me. He was the voice of reason, the schedule maker, and the one who had everything in order. I don't know if he had a touch of OCD—okay, he was OCD—but whatever I lacked, he had. For him the pregnancy was a shocker, and though it was a serious left turn from the few years we intended to spend before thinking of starting a family, he came around, flashed his trademark smile, and let me know he was excited that we were going to be parents.

PART FIVE

Mommyhood

1

....

FOR THE FIRST three months, I kept the news of my pregnancy a secret from everyone except my immediate family and a couple close friends. We wanted to keep this as private as possible for the first trimester.

These days, my life is a running conversation on Twitter; I share details about my day or post questions about the issues I'm dealing with to my two million followers, and they respond similarly. I like the give-and-take, and also the connection to a larger community. I look forward to the information and support there. But in the early months of my pregnancy Twitter hadn't been invented, and if it had been, I wouldn't have tweeted, "Hey, I'm four days pregnant!"

You hoped for the best during those precarious first three months, but you never knew. That's what made keeping the news quiet, other than to a few close girlfriends that I knew could keep a secret, such a unique period. I was excited and nervous, depending on the sensations I experienced as a new life developed inside me. The girlfriends I shared the news with were parents, and they were great to talk to about becoming a new mom.

Thank goodness it takes nine months to have a baby. Can you imagine the havoc if it happened instantly? I needed every minute of those nine months to contemplate the changes ahead, read books, learn about what was happening with my body, commune with Charlie, create a nursery, and prepare for the biggest responsibility of my life. I went through stages, though at the beginning I simply tried to adjust to the idea that I was going to be someone's mom, and that Charlie was going to be a dad (for the second time); we were going to be parents. Would we be good parents? Would I be a good mom? What would my baby be like? Would it be healthy? Would I be a room mother one day? My questions were endless.

At times, I found myself thinking about it in a cosmic sense, the way you do when you realize bringing a child into the world connects you to the larger picture of motherhood, all the generations that had come before you and the jobs they've done to raise their children. I also did my share of self-centered navel-gazing and wondering how my stomach was actually going to fit a baby. But I knew many women had done this before me.

One thing I did do immediately was, on the day I found out I was pregnant, I began putting shea butter on my belly, breasts, hips, and thighs to prevent stretch marks. With all that grease, I ruined my share of bedsheets. But guess what? No stretch marks! As for the traditional side effects of pregnancy, I had them. Early on, I battled serious fatigue. I'd be driving and want to pull over and take a nap. I feared something was wrong. But my mom and my doctor assured me this was normal. My body was telling me to slow down.

My biggest challenge was morning sickness, or the thought of it. I was nauseous a few mornings or it was just in my head. I just hoped and prayed I wouldn't puke due to a lifelong phobia of throwing up. I know—it's bizarre. And for the longest time, I had no idea why I was afflicted. I'd run out of the room if someone was sick. I didn't want to catch it. Or I'd ask if the person had the flu or food poisoning and hope it was the latter. I was in my early twenties before my mom explained that as a little girl I followed my dad into the bathroom while he was sick and saw him puke. I thought he was dying, she said, and it affected the rest of my life.

It pisses me off that something I don't even remember has had such an impact on me, but it has, and my phobia, formally known as emetophobia, presented a unique challenge during my first trimester. In theory, I don't think fear should ever hold people back from something they want to do, and I wasn't about to let my fear ruin the initial months of my pregnancy, when my body was changing as a result of the miracle taking place in my belly. As I said, I was challenged. My mom had had terrible morning sickness with her pregnancies, and my sister had puked with hers, too. I hoped and prayed my experience would be different, and it was. But it was a matter of mind over body, not a lack of nausea, and my methods weren't anything you're going to find in *What to Expect When You're Expecting*.

No, when I was hit with a wave of nausea, I'd say, "Bitch, get ahold of yourself. It's just in your head." I also ate tons of lemon Popsicles after hearing that lemon calmed an upset stomach. I heard the same about ginger candy, and despite burning the hell out of my throat, I popped them into my mouth like vitamins. I also had crackers and soda next to my bed at all times. But really, saying "Bitch, get ahold of yourself" was most effective.

My sense of taste and smell also changed. I loved salmon and usually ate it a couple times a week, but once I got pregnant, I couldn't even smell it without feeling my stomach turn. To this day I still can't eat salmon. The same was true of broccoli, my favorite vegetable. (The good news is that I can now eat broccoli.) Also the scent of a certain Dyptique candle called Mimosa, which I'd enjoyed for years (still can't smell that crap!) made me sick. I do enjoy other scents by Dyptique. As for cravings, I reached for the pickles. I couldn't get enough of them. And I ate ice cream almost every night before bed. Such weird, random things, but in looking back, I think they were God's way of warning that life was going to change with a child and I'd better learn to deal. I'd have to give up some favorite things, but I'd discover new pleasures. It makes sense.

I worked out all through my pregnancy. I got in my cardio on the elliptical, lifted light weights, and did lots of walking. My doctor told me not to get my heart rate up past 140, so I bought a heart monitor and didn't push it. In general, I learned to listen to my body and only did what felt good, a good rule to follow all the time, not just when you're pregnant.

By August, Charlie was working on his first season of *Two and a Half Men*. Unlike movies, sitcoms allow for pretty regular hours, which is convenient if you have a family, and is the reason many actors look for jobs on TV series. But as with any project, early on the sitcom led to long, hard days as everyone searched for the right notes. The network was doing everything it could to give the show a big launch, and between getting it right on camera and with promotion, Charlie put in extremely long hours. We didn't see each other as much as we had over the past year, but there was a payoff. *Two and a Half Men* was an instant hit, and we added to the celebratory mood by releasing a statement about our own wonderful news. It felt as if the sun were shining directly on us. Things couldn't have been better.

But can things be too good? Is there truth in the adage about something being too good to be true? I don't think so. I try to live in the moment, and in the same way, I don't worry about what's in the past. This took some time for me to figure out. I don't want to be one of those people who ask, "What if?" I think about what I have to do that day, and now that I have two kids, I relish those wonderful, easy daily moments; they go so fast. Everyone has his or her share of moments when the sky darkens and the storm sirens wail. Sometimes you bring the problems on yourself, while other times it's simply fate and the path we are chosen to be on.

In my case, it was definitely beyond my control. I had just been cast in *Elvis Has Left the Building*, a comedic road picture starring Kim Basinger and John Corbett, and I was telling my friends that director Joel Zwick should be acknowledged as an enlightened male in Hollywood for sticking with an actress who was four months pregnant, when that first storm cloud rolled in. My mom was diagnosed with kidney (renal cell) cancer. My mom called and matter-of-factly gave me the details of her diagnosis (doctors thought it was stage 2, an early stage). She filled me in on her surgery that was being scheduled, as well as her reassuring rationale that life had to go on despite this curveball. "And it will go on," she said defiantly, to all of us, including herself. Now, I'm sure privately with my dad this news crushed her, but her speech was my mom being strong for her family. She was our rock and that's how she handled bad news. Charlie offered similar words of support, and at my mom's urging, I made two trips to the movie's location in Santa Fe, New Mexico. It was hard going away, but it let me focus on something other than the scary situation she faced. I could feel my tummy growing tighter and my body changing yet again as I entered the midpoint of my second trimester. Amazing. Even more miraculous, I thought, was the timing of my mom's cancer with my pregnancy, something I continued to think about years later as I began healing. That she would get this diagnosis at the same time I was creating a new life struck me as extraordinary intersection of fate. I wanted to see meaning in it, but I couldn't think too much about it. As I was growing up, my mom would at times tell me with every death, there is a birth. I had to get that out of my head. (Ironically, two weeks before my mom died, my youngest nephew was born. Since I believe children choose their parents, I wanted to believe they also had something to do with the timing of their arrival in the world.) When I called to check on my mom at that time, she ended up asking about me. I was more amazed by this sense of selflessness when I looked back years later, yet it wasn't so much selflessness as it was the force of motherhood, a power I'd come to know. As much as she was looking forward to being a grandmother again, she was still being a mom to me and taking pleasure in seeing me prepare for this new role myself. We had wonderful conversations.

I made two trips to Santa Fe, and before the first one, I had an ultrasound and the doctor said Charlie and I could find out the baby's sex if we wanted. We weren't sure if we wanted to know. It's one of life's great surprises, yet modern technology and the urge to decorate a nursery before the baby arrives, along with the lure of curiosity, have made this information hard to resist. Charlie and I compromised. We had the doctor write it down on a piece of paper and put it in an envelope, which we then stuck in a drawer at home while we debated whether we wanted to know ahead of time. We lasted only a few days before we opened the envelope and found out we were having a girl. I was ecstatic. I told my mom right away. "I can't wait to buy pink everything," I said, sounding as giddy as a little girl myself.

I finished the movie, we got past my mom's first surgery, and then the holidays came and went. Christmas was spent with my parents during the day and Charlie's in the evening. We did a lot of driving, and those hours spent on the road might have been symbolic as we hit a couple bumpy roads in our relationship during these months. They were little things that I assumed couples go through. I chalked it up to stress and sensitivity. I was worried about my mom, Charlie was distracted with his new show. I was pregnant. We were getting ready to be new parents. It was an exciting time, but one filled with change and challenges.

I looked forward to decorating the nursery. With our house still mostly done in bachelor-pad black, I had a feeling this oasis of pink, as I envisioned it, was going to be my favorite room— and it was. I put a calming pink color on the walls (Benjamin Moore paint #883), hardwood floors with a beautiful rug, a crib, a changing table, and a twin bed with mermaid-themed bedding. It was pink galore, a little baby girl's fantasy room. No, make that a thirty-two-year-old girl's fantasy room. I loved it. Everything was set for her arrival.

Like many first-time moms, I may have been a little overzealous. I thought I needed everything imaginable for a baby—and needed it right away. I soon learned how simple a baby's needs are. They don't need all the fancy-schmancy stuff. Now I tell first-time mommies to keep it simple: diapers, bassinet, onesies, and a lot of love. My best advice? Relax and enjoy every moment.

Charlie and I had one last major detail to figure out—her name. My favorites were Lilly and Stella, something girly and feminine. Charlie had his heart set on Sam. Not Samantha. Just Sam. I wasn't easily sold, and we were still debating it when I had my baby shower. Mindy Weiss hosted the shower at the Hotel Bel-Air, and when my mom, Michelle, Charlie's mom and his sister, and all my friends arrived at the all-girl luncheon, they were each given a pastel-colored baby block with their initial on it. Toward the end of the shower, which was festive and fun, Charlie showed up and noticed three blocks were left over. Guess what the letters on them spelled? S-A-M. I kid you not. "How can you argue with that?" asked Charlie. Laughingly, I couldn't.

Charlie had named his angel.

2

....

TO CHRONICLE THE advancing stages of my pregnancy, we took photos of my belly from the side. The progress was unmistakable. As I headed into my final few months, everything I read about in the stack of books on my bedside table was coming true. I couldn't see my damn feet. It was the weirdest thing. And trying to shave my legs was incredibly difficult, an exercise in stretching and contortion. "Thank God I'm really flexible," I'd tell my mom and sister. I continued getting my bikini wax; my sister thought I'd lost my mind when she heard that newsflash. It's painful enough under normal circumstances, but pregnant, whoa, it's a new level of horrendous! You're incredibly sensitive down there, but as I explained to Michelle, I didn't give a shit. I'd rather suffer through that few minutes of pain.

I also had a dark line down the center of my belly. I still have no idea why there is a dark line, and let me tell you, it takes a long time for it to go away. Another side effect of that little peanut getting bigger was major heartburn. My mom warned me, but it didn't make the burning sensation any more tolerable. Just drinking water ignited that irritating fire in my chest. Thankfully, it went away as soon as the baby was born.

Such pleasant stuff, right?

It got better. We found out I needed a C-section. Having been present when my sister gave birth naturally, and having watched the baby come out of her, I wasn't terribly disappointed at skipping a vaginal birth. No matter which way the baby came out, though, it was hard to imagine—and scary. The doctor picked Wednesday, March 10, as her birthday; Charlie was going to be on hiatus; it was also the day closest to my actual due date when the doctor scheduled C-sections. However, as he said, it was really up to Sam.

In anticipation of the big occasion, Charlie informed me he'd gotten me a special commemorative gift and had it engraved with Sam's scheduled birthday. I told Mr. Organized that Sam might not be born on the tenth. "What do you mean?" he said. "We scheduled it on the tenth." I laughed. "It's not really up to us," I said. "She could come earlier." He thought I was crazy.

On the morning of the ninth, Charlie and I completed the paperwork for the hospital and I had my final checkup. The doctor said everything was fine and normal and he'd see me the next day. Stupidly I hadn't mentioned during my checkup that I didn't feel quite right. I chalked it up to nervousness, and when my doctor asked how I was feeling, I said, "Fine." For our last night as a couple, Charlie and I had planned dinner at our favorite restaurant, Giorgio's, and I was looking forward to the meal. Until then, we were just hanging out together.

But as the day progressed, I started to feel worse. At one point, I was on the phone with my mom and told her to hold on because I was having a stomach cramp—or so I told her. Now, I know better. It was a contraction. I was in labor. I was also in denial. I have a high tolerance for pain, and I thought I could suck whatever it was up, get through the night, and make it until our scheduled appointment in the morning. Why the stubbornness? Maybe some of Charlie's obsession with sticking to a schedule had rubbed off on me.

After Charlie saw me struggle down the stairs, he asked what was wrong, and I had to tell him that I was having seriously bad pains. His face went white when I said they'd been going on since early morning, but had recently increased in both frequency and severity. He called the doctor, who told him to bring me in right away. To Charlie, that meant get in the car and go. As far as I was concerned, though, right away meant after I took a shower and washed my hair. Again, I don't understand my thought process.

My parents on their
wedding day.

My second-grade
school picture.

With my mom,
grandpa, and sister.

My sister and me at Grandma's.
I loved high heels from
an early age.

Kissing Michelle outside our house in Mokena, Illinois.

Camping trip with my dad and Michelle. I'm in the center.

Our house in Mokena.

Our house in Downers Grove.

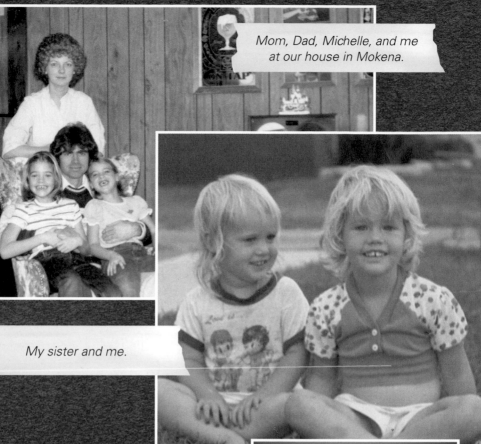

Mom, Dad, Michelle, and me at our house in Mokena.

My sister and me.

James and me.

My First Communion.

High school prom.

With Kirstie Alley on the set
of Drop Dead Gorgeous.

Pat and me in 2000.

My sister's wedding day—
I did her hair and makeup.

*On the set of
Starship Troopers.*

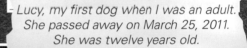

*— Lucy, my first dog when I was an adult.
She passed away on March 25, 2011.
She was twelve years old.*

*Christmas at my parents'
house with Charlie.*

*Charlie and me in Hawaii in
2001—our first trip together.*

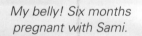

Charlie and me on our wedding day, taking a private moment to soak it all in.

My belly! Six months pregnant with Sami.

With my mom and baby Sami.

Pregnant with Lola on Easter, one month after I filed for divorce.

Sami meeting her baby sister for the first time.

Lola and me in the hospital.

My beautiful girls and me.

Sami and Lola, sisters and best friends.

Richie and me at his parents' house.

With my girls while filming It's Complicated.

Backstage with my sexy Dancing with the Stars costar Gilles.

Promoting It's Complicated.

Sami & Lola,
I arrived here fine, I will be
in your life morning, noon &
Night. When you think of me, I
will be there to protect you
from harm always.
Love
Nana forever ♡

A note for my girls left by their Nana.

Nor do I know how I made it through the shower and shampoo. I had to sit on the floor while I blew my hair dry. I was in such pain the dogs stared at me with concern. I can't believe I thought I could make it through the night. I guess I desperately wanted to make sure Sam was born on the tenth and Charlie's gift was engraved with the real date. A part of me thought maybe this was all in my head and I wasn't really in labor. Chalk it up to irrationality. By that point I just didn't want to have the baby in the car.

Charlie sped to the hospital. Since we had not taken any Lamaze classes, we had no idea what to do. Every time I winced through a contraction, he told me to "breathe!" I barely heard him. I withdrew inside myself and dealt with the pain rolling through me. I'll tell you, though, it's amazing more men aren't injured during those moments. Contractions are a pain I have never experienced before. Women are not exaggerating when they say this. It's bad, and this is coming from someone who had her chest cut open a few times. This was painful. Charlie dropped me off in front of the hospital, then parked the car and probably had a cigarette to calm his nerves.

Inside, I was quickly admitted and taken to the maternity floor, where a nurse hooked me up to a monitor and confirmed that I was in labor. I was relieved. It wasn't all in my head! My contractions were six minutes apart. Charlie was asked to step out of the room while I got an epidural. The relief was quick, but let me tell you, what an odd sensation. When it kicked in, I wasn't able to feel my legs, and I hated that. For a split second I thought, what if that never wears off? It was a little scary, scary for the fear of the unknown. I had never had a baby before and was experiencing all of this for the first time. I thought, if it was that bad, women wouldn't keep having children.

As they wheeled me into the operating room, I glanced over at my husband and thought he looked sexy in his scrubs. I actually wanted him to bring them home. Just before 11:00 p.m., our daughter was born. Sam J. Sheen—her middle initial stands for both of our moms, Joni and Janet—weighed in at a healthy seven pounds three ounces and sounded delighted to have arrived in this world. In one of my most vivid and happiest memories, Charlie intercepted her as the doctor handed her off to the nurse, to show his parents, who were waiting outside. It was too soon. She wasn't even properly cleaned, weighed, and swaddled. But he was so excited and proud of his "little princess," as he called her.

My mom and dad came up the next morning. I overflowed with joy as my mom met her new granddaughter; she was so happy. My mom loved being a grandma more than anything else in the world. The moment I held my baby daughter for the first time, I felt a love I had never before felt. It's different from loving your husband, or boyfriend or girlfriend. I can't explain it. It was magical! In those first few hours and days you are simply the happiest person on the planet. At least I was. I spent four days in the hospital recovering from my C-section and nursing the baby. Charlie slept there every night, too, and seeing him with our baby made me fall more in love with him, and he voiced the same. We were parents, together. We were a family, not just husband and wife but a family of three. During the day, he went home for a bit, and always with a baby blanket we stole from the hospital (I'm sure we actually paid for it). All the books said if you have dogs, bring home a blanket with the baby's scent on it. We had the dogs sleep with it to get used to her smell.

Charlie and I were both ready when we finally got the green light to take Sam home to see her new room and meet her furry siblings. Our initial adjustment to family life was marred by an unexpected glitch. Throughout my pregnancy, friends repeatedly advised us to hire a baby nurse. Charlie and I were far from incompetent or unprepared; in fact, we were at the other extreme, overprepared. And truth be told, I was against hiring any help. I was breast-feeding and unsure what a nurse might do. I was confused by this.

But people were so adamant about our needing a baby nurse that we were scared to not have one, especially Charlie, who was sold on the idea the first time someone mentioned the nurse would stay up all night to make sure the baby breathed normally. I had to remember I'd married a man who had a bulletproof bedroom door and a fire pole in the closet for an emergency escape. He was always prepared for a disaster.

Even though my mom stayed with us for two weeks, turning that time into a heavenly, much-treasured experience by cooking for us, getting up in the night with Sam and me, talking to me as I nursed my baby, and bringing me water and pretzels (nursing made me thirsty and hungry), we still hired a baby nurse. I had to put Charlie at ease. The nurse was from Brazil, and I wish I had good things to say about her. But on her first night with us, she sat on the twin bed across from me as I nursed Sam and stared at me while flipping through magazines. I didn't like having her there. I'm not that shy with my body, but this was such an intimate moment of me bonding with my daughter that I felt self-conscious.

The next night, she came in and went to bed. She actually got into the twin bed in the nursery and went to sleep. I hadn't even put the baby down in the crib for the night. Charlie was pissed. We had hired her to watch the baby to make sure she was breathing all night. How was she going to do that if she was sleeping herself? We also found out she wasn't a licensed nurse. That was it for her. Two nights. She was so fired.

After a couple of weeks, the three of us settled into a nice routine. Charlie was back at work, and I handled mommy duties. Every day was a new adventure, with hours spent marveling at my baby girl as she ate, slept, and stared up at me with large, inquisitive eyes. Night feedings didn't bother me; I loved that quiet time with her. It was special. I'd tell every new mother to savor these moments. I know it gets exhausting, but it sure does go fast. I knew I wouldn't be able to get that time back so I really enjoyed it.

One thing that I wasn't prepared for were night sweats. For me, the sweat was out of control. I couldn't believe that much water came out of my body. My hair would be soaked when I woke up in the morning. It was disgusting, but part of the process—and it eventually passed.

The human body is amazing, especially a woman's body. At times during my pregnancy and then post-baby, I was amazed at what your body can go through. A new life grew inside me, my body expanded, the baby came out of me, and then I provided nourishment. Talk about miracles.

I felt good for having taken care of myself during my pregnancy. Among the more pleasant surprises was how quickly I began to lose the thirty pounds I'd put on during my pregnancy. Nursing helped. Because of the C-section, I couldn't exercise for six weeks, but I didn't feel like hitting the gym yet. I was too damn tired, and I wanted to deal with other issues first.

3

....

ALTHOUGH CHARLIE DOTED on Sam, which I adored seeing, I hated that the two of us continued to encounter bumps in our relationship. We started experiencing these bumps more frequently, and I wasn't sure why.

I think a lot of women can relate to how, when things aren't quite right in your relationship, you blame yourself. It can affect your self-esteem, and that's exactly what happened with me.

A progression of incidents, which I won't go into in detail, started to make me feel vulnerable and confused. Then, a couple months after having Sam, I received an offer from *Playboy*. It wasn't the first time they'd asked me to pose in the magazine. As I mentioned earlier, I began hearing from them as soon as I finished *Wild Things*. But this time was different, and I thought maybe I should say yes.

Why was it different? I had various reasons. I wanted people to see that a woman could still be sexy after having a baby. I wanted my husband to think I looked sexy. I wanted to feel sexy myself. I was starting to feel insecure and thought maybe this would help. In addition, I said to myself, "One day they aren't going to ask you, so you might as well do it now."

Before responding to the magazine, I asked Charlie. At first he didn't express much support, but after talking to me and thinking about it, he changed his mind, explaining that as a long-time fan of the magazine he'd be a hypocrite if he said no. Had he objected, of course, I would've turned it down. But as soon as he offered his support, I accepted the offer. Then *Playboy* surprised us by asking Charlie to take the pictures. I wasn't sure, but I thought the last time that might've happened was when John Derek famously photographed his wife, Bo.

Although flattered, Charlie declined, good-naturedly explaining he couldn't guarantee they'd be in focus. Privately, we also thought it might be too intimate, though I have to admit, once I was committed, a part of me thought it would be cool if Charlie was the photographer. How great to have your husband show you off that intimately to the rest of the world, or maybe that wouldn't be so great. Regardless, the pictures needed to be in focus, so we decided not to have him do it.

Anyway, I went with the photographer the magazine recommended and then had numerous meetings about the shoot. We worked out the details (no vajayjay), the concept (beach), the location (the Bahamas), and the wardrobe (not much).

In the meantime, I booked a Lifetime movie, *I Do (But I Don't)*, with Dean Cain, an old friend of mine from when I was starting out and had a tiny part on an episode of *Lois & Clark: The New Adventures of Superman*. I wanted to shoot the movie first to give me some time to lose my baby weight (I had ten pounds to go!). With Sam only three months old, I had mixed feelings about going back to work sooner than I anticipated. At the level where I was at in my career, a longer leave would make it that much harder to get a job. My agent advised me to get back to work, so I did!

Charlie and I still didn't have a nanny. So I had to figure out how I was going to film a movie without a nanny. My mom visited often and helped me, and I took Sam everywhere. Unfortunately, my mom wasn't physically ready after her surgery to go with me to Montreal for the movie, but I thought, I'll handle this myself, and I did for a short time. I couldn't believe how much crap I had to pack for me and the baby!

Thank God Dean was on my flight. A good daddy himself, he helped lug some of my bags as we went through customs. I had my arms full with an infant. Once settled and on the set, I felt good about being back at work. I love the job, I love acting, I love focusing on a new character, and I love the camaraderie of the cast and crew. It was a welcome escape from the issues at home—and having my daughter there made me even happier.

During filming, I set up a Pack 'n Play next to me and prayed Sam would not cry during a scene. Since I still nursed, I had to double up on the breast pads to prevent any leaks on my wardrobe. (Sorry, it's the truth.) Between feedings, burpings, spit-ups, cries, naps, and dirty diapers, and clean clothes, I juggled a lot between takes. I finally realized I needed help. When Charlie got a break, I asked him to give me a hand, and he brought our housekeeper and left her there when he had to go back so I'd have an extra set of hands. He ended up flying back and forth several times.

Back in L.A., Charlie also focused on the remodeling we were doing on a new house we had bought just before I left. Yes, the house. We'd envisioned a home that would be ours, one where we could raise a family, and following weeks of searching, we found one we thought was perfect. It was close to the studio where Charlie worked on *Two and a Half Men* and was beautiful, with plenty of rooms and a yard for the brood of children and animals we envisioned. It was, in fact, the old Al Jolson estate in Encino. But it should be called the divorce house. I'm not joking. We bought it from Katey Sagal (divorced there), who purchased it from Kirstie Alley (divorced there), and we found out three other couples before her also split while living there. And guess what? We also got divorced living in that damn house! So if you're married and in the market for a home in Encino, California, I would pass on the Al Jolson estate.

After having a blast on the movie with Dean Cain, I headed back to L.A. and did an almost immediate turnaround for the Bahamas. Five months had passed since I had given birth, and my body had bounced back into shape. Though I didn't have a huge amount of time to work out, filming and caring for the baby kept me busy, and apparently burned calories. I wasn't at my pre-baby weight, but I felt good physically, and I was confident about the shoot.

Well, I had no choice actually. If we waited any longer, it would be hurricane season and I'd already committed to the shoot, so my body was what it was. So off I went.

4

....

TOO BAD CHARLIE had started the second season of *Two and a Half Men*. Otherwise he could've come along. In his stead, I had a mini-entourage that included Sam, my mom, my dad (yes, my dad), my hairdresser (Campbell), and my makeup artist (Lutz). Both were dear friends—and both had girlfriends, which made the thought of them seeing me naked kind of awkward. They treated me like I was their little sister. Again, awkward. But I told myself to get used to it and focus on having fun.

And fun was my goal. I was thrilled about being able to take my parents and let them have nice vacation. On the way to the Bahamas, we barely made our connecting flight in Miami, then once on the plane, we hit a series of delays, including a heavy thunder and lightning storm that delayed takeoff, a problem with the ground crew, and then Sam had a meltdown. Ours was the last flight of the day, and I prayed we'd take off because I didn't want to try to find some place for all of us to sleep.

Fortunately, there was a break in the weather and we got to the Bahamas. Unfortunately, my bags did not. Everybody else got his or her luggage except me. My mom joked that I was going to be naked the whole trip anyway and didn't need my clothes. At least I had a toothbrush in my carry-on, and in the morning she and I bought me a bathing suit, underwear, and a sarong in the hotel gift shop.

Later that morning, I remembered an incident from my childhood that made this whole episode ironic. When my sister and I were kids, we found an issue of my dad's *Playboy*—he had a subscription—and Michelle and I cried to him, thinking he and my mom were getting divorced. He explained that he only had the magazine for the articles. We believed him and felt relieved. He laughed when I reminded him of that. I know it might be weird to bring my parents, especially my dad, on a shoot for *Playboy*, but they weren't at the actual shoot. They were poolside, baby!

Even though Lutz, Campbell, and I wanted to have fun in the sun, we were there to work. My mornings were spent with Lutz and Campbell coming to my room for breakfast and getting me ready. Then I kissed the baby good-bye, left her with my parents, and took a boat to a remote island where we shot hundreds of photos. It was well after sundown by the time we got back to the hotel. You would think having done *Wild Things* would make posing for *Playboy* easier. Actually it was a little harder. It was bright sunlight out in the wide open for anyone on a boat to see me. Also I was posing by myself, nobody else to kind of be there, too. On the boat that first morning, I thought, what the hell am I doing? It was typical me. To have a flash of that thought, in a situation where I felt vulnerable. I also had to get that thought out of my head so I could do a good job.

I knew there was no turning back. Nor did I ever really have second thoughts. I'd made a commitment and I was going to suck it up and do whatever was necessary to do a great job. That's me in a nutshell—a girl who keeps her word, stays focused, and tries hard.

Once on the island, I saw the largest piece of clothing they had for me consisted of a few strands of seaweed. It was a shock-

ing reminder that I wasn't going to be wearing much of anything. But seaweed? It wasn't even real clothing. Oh, well. It
wasn't the time to dwell on feeling insecure about taking off my
clothes. With a job to do, I channeled a bunch of positive energy
and threw on my seaweed. I said to myself, "Okay, as long as
you're doing this, make it great."

I declined the pitcher of margaritas they had waiting. It was
too hot to drink and I thought, getting tipsy, this could go all
bad. I wanted to keep my wits about me. Quite frankly, Lutz
and Campbell needed a drink more than I did. They could barely
look at me without blushing, though after a few hours and various setups, all of us got more comfortable. Indeed, soon Lutz
was rubbing oil on my breasts and ice cubes on my nipples.
Playboy liked hard nipples (sorry, maybe TMI), and Campbell,
in a stroke of creative genius, braided some bamboo leaves in my
hair, which looked fantastic. His best styling tool for my hair?
The salt water. Honest to God, it was amazing.

I lost my inhibition in the middle of day two when a boat
went by with a bunch of people. Initially, I covered myself up,
and then I thought, girl, there is going to be more than a boat-
load of people looking at you topless! I dropped the cover-up
and said, "Let's keep going." By the end, I felt good about the
photo shoot. Oh, and my luggage finally showed up!

Back home, *Playboy* sent me the proof sheet so I could ap-
prove those I liked. Who better to help pick the best shots than
my husband? Charlie and I edited the pictures together. Although my most private area was contractually off-limits, I actually approved one black-and-white photo that showed my hoo
hah. It was my favorite shot of the bunch. To me, the whole

shoot looked editorial, stylized, sexy, and natural, and I loved that it was black-and-white, which *Playboy* ran only rarely.

Sooner rather than later, the world was going to see me naked. With the vajayjay shot, I didn't think there was anything more I could possibly expose about myself. I was wrong.

5

....

ABOUT A MONTH later, I noticed Charlie staring at me, his piercing dark eyes fastened on me with an unusual intensity. It was early October, and the two of us were in the kitchen, talking about the progress on the work being done on the new house. I stopped making lunch and asked why he was looking at me like that. I didn't understand. He'd recently seen two thousand photos of me butt naked. What had he missed?

"You're pregnant, aren't you?" he said, so sure I barely noticed he was asking me a question.

"What are you talking about? I'm not pregnant." I meant that, too. As far as I knew, I wasn't pregnant. We had definitely talked about a sibling, but I certainly didn't think I would get pregnant so quick after having Sam.

"Yes, you are," he said.

"No, I'm not. I'd know if I was. Why are you saying that?"

"Because you just put pickles on your sandwich. I've only seen you eat pickles one time—when you were pregnant with Sam."

He had a point, but I laughed it off. Charlie was full of superstitions, intuitive predications and declarations, and far-fetched theories. However, at a birthday party for a friend's child the following weekend, I was overcome with a sudden wave of dizziness, a feeling that was more strange than faint, like a full-body reboot. I looked across the room at Charlie and thought, damn, he might be right.

On the way home, I had Charlie stop at the pharmacy and get me a pregnancy test. I told him to pick up five. "Just in case," I said. He came back with one. He knew we didn't need any more. Indeed, a short time later, we were staring at the results. I hadn't even missed my period. "I knew it," he said. "It was the pickles."

I was surprised at how easily I got pregnant again. I know: if you don't use birth control, chances are you'll get pregnant. But at the time, quite a few of my girlfriends were trying for their second baby and having a difficult time getting pregnant. Charlie and I weren't trying, but we weren't *not* trying. Ideally, we wanted our babies close in age. Charlie's siblings are all close, and my sister and I are only eighteen months apart. I was grateful it happened easily.

Charlie was excited about baby number two. Both of us were. I was nervous again about throwing up, but I employed the same mind-over-nausea tactics I did the first time around. Charlie and I seemed to have hit a groove. I felt that we were very connected. Our recent rough patch was behind us, and I chalked it up to the bumps that every marriage hits. We worked through it. Those types of challenges would only make us stronger, I thought. And closer. I was in it for the long haul.

In November, we moved into our new home and settled in as

much as possible despite the chaos of unpacking and workmen still finishing the remodel. I guest-starred on Charlie's show. I had also done an episode when I was pregnant with Sam and they'd covered my belly. This time my character came back *with* a baby. The producers hired twins for the part, but Charlie and I thought it would be cute if we put Sam in the role and had that memory of her. But I'll never forget being in the makeup room, not wanting anyone to know I was pregnant again, yet getting terribly sick to my stomach from the smell of incense burning nearby. It took extraordinary willpower to not barf while getting my hair and makeup done. The payoff was the episode: it was funny, and I loved working with Charlie.

Shortly after, our marriage changed drastically. It came out of the blue, and it was more than a rough patch. These issues are so personal that I don't want to divulge exactly what changes, and if you've ever been through a similar situation, you know the details don't matter. The fact is, our marriage was crumbling, and fast.

I was an emotional wreck, careering up and down and in every other direction. Some days I was sad, confused, angry, shocked, and full of despair; and other days I ignored the situation, marching forward in a daze of denial. They were days of denial, too. My *Playboy* issue came out and I promoted it on *The Tonight Show* and *The Ellen DeGeneres Show*, smiling and joking to keep from revealing that my personal life was in shambles. But the façade was hard to maintain. Charlie and I pulled out of a scheduled *Redbook* magazine cover shoot after having an argument at the last minute. We couldn't blame it on my pregnancy since no one knew it yet. I don't remember what our publicist told the magazine. We ended up rescheduling, and it turned out to be one of my favorite pictures the two of us took. It also turned out to be the last photo shoot we did together.

We kept the pregnancy quiet until I got through my first trimester, though there was a scare along the way. At nine weeks, I encountered some bleeding, not a lot but enough to concern my doctor, who had me meet him at his office on a Sunday. He gave me some medication to help stop the bleeding. I was worried we'd lose the baby. I blamed myself. I wondered if the stress of my marriage had caused the problem. Since I hadn't had any problems with my first pregnancy, I figured it had to be the stress. I tried to relax and take it easy for a few weeks, but my personal life did not make either one a simple task.

At my next ultrasound appointment, I was terrified I wouldn't see a heartbeat. I was a basket case as I lay on the examining table, pulled up my shirt, and felt the chill of the gel spread on my tummy. Thankfully, a moment later, I bravely turned my head toward the ultrasound screen and saw the tiny heart beating normally. "Everything looks perfect," my doctor said. I thought, wow, I'm blessed with a fighter; this baby is strong. Little did I know how much strength she'd give me in months to come.

Toward the end of December the situation at home worsened, which was hard to believe, and I left late at night, taking Sam, and we moved back into our old house. I guess it was a cooling-off period for us. After four days I went back home.

In January, Charlie and I attended the Golden Globes together. He was nominated again. I wore a beautiful dress and stood by my husband's side, smiling and supporting him as if everything were picture-perfect. We looked like a solid couple.

Unfortunately, Charlie didn't win that night, and we left early; it was not a good night for us.

The Screen Actors Guild Awards, in February, was another hard evening, but for different reasons. I was now five months pregnant and not feeling like myself. Charlie and I were late getting out the door when I put on a beautiful burgundy gown that a stylist had found for me and had altered for my growing belly. It didn't fit. I turned to a friend who was helping me get ready and gritted my teeth. I threw open my closet door. "What do I have in here that will fit—and that's appropriate?" I said.

I didn't want to go, but I feared the press would speculate we were having problems if I wasn't with Charlie. In hindsight, we simply could have said I wasn't feeling well if anyone asked. But I wasn't thinking like my normal self. I had hormones raging through my body, and I was trying to figure out what to do about my marriage. My frustration came to a head over that dress. I was close to tears but didn't want to ruin my makeup. Talk about your silly problems, right?

Well, with my friend's help and reassurance, I finally pulled a black Dolce & Gabbana dress out of my closet. It was stretchy and the only thing I could get on that would remotely look good for an awards show. I apologized to my friend for being unusually self-conscious. But it takes a lot of effort to put a look together for these events, and after getting into the outfit, I felt underdressed, not to mention I thought I looked like a sausage squeezed into that thing.

I did not relish the idea of walking the red carpet in front of a thousand reporters and photographers. Ah, well, the event wasn't about me; it was about Charlie, who was nominated. My job was to suck it up, smile, and support my husband, which I gamely did.

The photos of us on the red carpet that night were the last pictures taken of us at a public event together. A short time later, Charlie and I split up. Those photos of us ran everywhere.

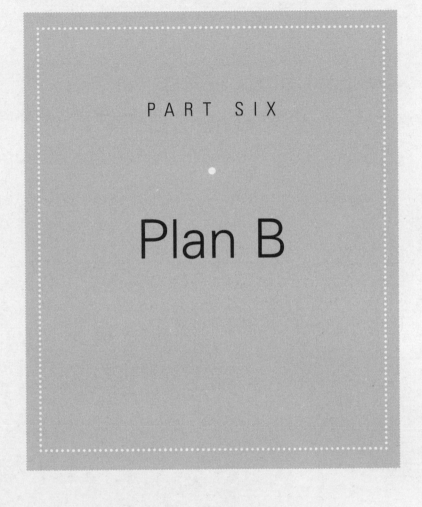

PART SIX

Plan B

1

....

THERE'S LIFE AS we imagine, fantasize, and hope it will turn out, and then there's real life, which is a constant exercise in dealing with unforeseen problems, fixing mistakes, regrouping, putting pieces back together, and turning to Plan B. Real life is made up of Plan Bs. Ask any parent who's planned an outing or a vacation only to have a child throw up and run a 103-degree fever an hour before you're scheduled to leave. That's when you go to Plan B. The same is true when you break off a relationship, stare into the mirror that first Saturday night alone, and ask yourself, "Now what?" Or you might be one of those office workers who share in a multimillion-dollar lottery superprize and don't need to work anymore. That's also a Plan B. I'm not advocating giving up dreams and fantasies. No, far from it. But it helps to recognize that the best-intentioned plans don't always work out the way you want. Life rarely works out the way we want, and that's when we turn to Plan B. A rainstorm in the middle of a family camping trip requires us to check into a nearby motel. That's Plan B. I remember the motels from my childhood as much as, if not more than, the camping trips they washed out. Those Plan Bs are what provide the fun, adventure, learning, growth, and wisdom. All of us have our own variations, or our stories, and if you're anything like me, you have your own example of trying to forestall the obvious need to turn to a Plan B. In my case, I didn't want to think of my marriage as over.

Although deep down I realized the finality, I spent days and nights wondering how Charlie and I had reached this point. Blame wasn't part of the equation. I loved him. He was the father of my children. It made me incredibly sad to think of where we were in our relationship, and I wished we could turn the clock back. I held on to hope that it wasn't over. I walked on eggshells, avoiding my husband, wishing the problems would magically disappear and we would go back to those bliss-filled days when we were newlyweds.

But we didn't, and I started to not feel like myself. Dark clouds filled the sky. I felt confused, angry, and hopeless. I'm normally a social person. I love having friends over to the house. I love to entertain. It doesn't have to be formal. My favorite times are when a girlfriend will drop by for coffee and we'll spend a few hours catching up. But I found myself declining invitations, avoiding calls, and closing myself off at home. I had a convenient excuse: I was busy with Sam, now nearly one, and I was almost six months pregnant.

When things aren't right in a relationship (or at work), it can change you in ways you don't necessarily like, but don't have the wherewithal to fix, and that was happening to me. I started to not like myself. I felt my spark disappearing. I was losing my zest for life. I wasn't me. I couldn't do anything about it until I was ready to confront the truth.

But I didn't want anyone to know Charlie and I had serious problems at home. I barely acknowledged it myself. That would've meant admitting the truth, and then I would've had to do something about it. Better to sail along in denial. As I said earlier, only my parents knew, and they were extremely concerned and worried. But out of respect they tried to not cross the line too much. When they did, I got defensive and pushed them away.

It was difficult, but as I told them, I had to work this out for myself. Charlie wasn't a boyfriend. He was my husband, my partner, the father of my children, and deciding to leave my marriage didn't just affect me. It affected him, our families, and our babies. I had a running debate in my head. Sometimes I shared my thoughts with my mom. Most of the time I kept my thoughts to myself. I knew one thing for sure: before making any move, I wanted to be absolutely sure I had explored every option and wasn't making a rash decision.

Actually, my thinking went even further. I didn't want to get divorced. Period. I didn't grow up in a divorced family and neither did Charlie. I remember talking to my mom one day as I played with Sam, my hand on my belly, feeling the baby move inside me, and I could literally feel my heart ache at the thought of divorce. "I'd like to try to make it," I told my mom.

For the first time in my life I reached out to a therapist. I wanted to speak with an unbiased person. Through friends, I found a woman who was lovely and patient and clearly knew her business. With a few pointed questions, she put me at ease and got me talking, then mostly listened to me. Interestingly, I ended up listening to myself, too. As I detailed my issues at home, I heard a rational woman expressing hurt, disappointment, confusion, concern, loneliness, sadness, and even fear. I knew I had to leave my marriage.

On several occasions, I nearly did. I came close. Each time, though, I got scared and changed my mind. I couldn't do it. Finally, I decided to stick it out until the baby was born. With only three months to go, I thought it was best to avoid putting any more pressure on myself. I could prepare for our child's arrival. Charlie and I still didn't know if we were having a boy or a girl. We'd decided this second time around to be surprised.

Another distraction came my way when I landed a small part in *Edmond*, a dark indie movie from David Mamet starring William H. Macy. It was a couple days of work in town, and my wardrobe fitting was at Trashy lingerie. I kid you not. I wore a bustier, fishnets, and stripper heels; and, no, my character was not pregnant in the film. I had a blast.

I also took cooking lessons from a professional chef who was a good friend of Charlie's and mine. I was still eating those plastic meals delivered and figured, I can't feed those to children, I need to cook! The chef came to the house two to three times a week and taught me a series of fabulous recipes. Sometimes my mom came over and cooked with us. I even made a few nice dinners for Charlie, who revealed flashes of the old Charlie, enough that we actually had some good moments that reminded me of how much I loved my husband, truly loved him.

And that's what made it so painful when I finally knew I had no alternative but to choose Plan B.

It happened after a night that will remain in my mind forever if for no other reason than I realized it was the end. There were other reasons, but they paled in comparison to the tremors that rattled my whole being as I saw that I had run out of alternatives and excuses. Everything exploded that night. I ended up sleeping in Sam's room—though I can't say I slept. I lay in the twin bed opposite her crib and stared into the darkness. I had never felt more alone and scared in my life. My face was drenched from tears. I replayed the argument I'd had with Charlie. I heard advice my parents had given me. I heard statements I'd made myself. Finally, as the first slivers of dawn broke through the night, I found myself looking at my daughter sleeping in her crib and I asked, "If this were Sami, what would you tell her to do?"

2

A FEW HOURS later, Charlie left for work. And soon after, with my heart pounding, I left for a hotel.

I'll never forget my scramble through the house. Shaking and terrified, I packed a suitcase, put my daughter in the car, and explained to our confused housekeeper why I wanted her to come, too. We went to the Beverly Hills Hotel. It was my first time back since Charlie had carried me through the door on our wedding night. But I didn't want to go to another hotel. I felt safe there and knew the hotel staff would make sure I was taken care of.

After getting settled, I called a lawyer and went straight to her office. I called on every ounce of strength and courage when it was time for me to actually sign the petition for divorce, the document that would be filed with the court. Memories of my brief but full marriage flashed in front of my eyes, starting with one in particular—that of Charlie and me signing the document to get married. I also recalled our first trip, our engagement, our first Christmas together, the birth of our daughter. In such a short time, we'd shared a big life.

Now, here I was, six months pregnant with our second child and putting an end to our marriage. It was a sad time. *Divorced.* The word resonated in my head like a church bell hitting a sour note. I left the lawyer's office feeling numb. Plan B, indeed.

I drove straight to a fitting for a pilot I'd booked, crying the whole time to my mom, whom I called as soon as I got in the car. I was devastated my marriage was over. The first thing I said was "I escaped the insanity." Somehow I managed to deal with my fitting as if nothing out of the ordinary had happened. I thought I was being controlled and professional by not letting my personal life interfere with my work. In reality, I was in shock that I'd actually gone through with it and frightened by not knowing what would happen next.

Afterward, one of my closest girlfriends came to the hotel to provide support and a much-needed shoulder. She brought a bottle of wine. "It's for me," she said. "I know you can't drink." We sat on the bed and talked for hours. I had the TV on in the background. At some point, I looked up and saw the news about my divorce on the CNN ticker. "Oh my God," I gasped. It was already in the media before Charlie received the paperwork. I felt terrible, as if my privacy had been invaded.

No one's asking me, but I think something is wrong with a court system that allows such intimate proceedings to be made public before the parties can deal with matters themselves, or even to be public at all.

I spent a lonely night in that hotel room bed, tossing and turning in a sea of upset and anxiety. I cried the whole time. I knew I'd made the right decision, but my heart ached for Charlie, our daughter, our unborn child, and our family.

The next day, as expected, the shit hit the fan. The divorce was all over the news, Charlie was calling and texting me, and hundreds of others, it seemed, were doing the same. In the midst of the storm, I made sure Sam and my housekeeper were set up in the hotel, then, believe it or not, I went to a table reading for my new pilot. Several people asked, why didn't I drop out of the project and deal with my life? I had a simple answer. Only a few people have the luxury of pulling over to the side to focus solely on one issue at a time; I wasn't one of them. Stuff happens every day to people and they still have to go to work. You deal the best you can. Reese Witherspoon can take time off from her career and jump back into amazing roles. At my level, I have to plug away. And I was plugging away. Hey, given the size of my belly, I was amazed to be working at all. Despite all the shit in my life, I was grateful to have a job.

At the table reading, I acted as if nothing had happened. I'm not one to air my dirty laundry to everyone. I figured most had heard that I filed; it was on every media outlet. I also didn't want the producers to worry that I was too distracted to deliver the performance they'd envisioned when they cast me.

Only those who've been through similar situations know the level of multitasking that was required to keep my life running so I could focus on doing a good job. Right before we shot the pilot, Charlie got an apartment and I moved back into our home. Ultimately, the pilot was a nice distraction. For a few hours a day, I could step out of myself and into a character that wasn't on the verge of becoming a single working mother of two children.

One of the biggest and most unanticipated problems I encountered was the paparazzi. They followed me everywhere. Following the initial shock of our divorce and a joint statement from Charlie and me, I thought the news would fade from the headlines and we could get on with our lives. I was wrong. Very wrong. It was the split that wouldn't die. I guess that I filed while six months pregnant gave the drama staying power. For the next three years, our split became a soap opera for every celebrity-media outlet, whether on the newsstand, TV, or online.

Some stories were true and some weren't. Most were full of speculation from unnamed sources and so-called "friends close to the couple." As hard as I tried my best to ignore the cover stories and articles, the attention turned a difficult situation into an embarrassing nightmare that I desperately wanted to disappear. I was horrified when reporters called about Sami's first birthday and paparazzi staked out her party. Everyone advised me to cancel it. But no way was I going to cancel her celebration because Charlie and I were going through our shit. The point was to make life better, not worse.

In hindsight, I should've either canceled or postponed it. Sami was too young to even remember the party, and I'm sure the majority of the guests were uncomfortable watching as Charlie pretended to be cool and calm while I powered through the party with a mama bear ferocity that would probably frighten me if I saw a tape of it today. Hey, I never claimed to be anything more than a work in progress.

That's the best advice I can offer. You must think of yourself, and your life, as a work in progress. For me, the next three months were exactly that, work, and often I wondered whether I could call any of it progress. I tried not to think too far ahead. When I did, I'd get overwhelmed. I took it day by day, sometimes hour by hour. I frequently got emotional thinking about how much had changed in a year. At times, I blamed myself for not doing more or trying harder, and other times I looked heavenward and asked, "What the hell happened?"

My mom came up more often to help me with Sami, I still took cooking lessons, my girlfriends would come over, and I doubled up on a great mommy-and-me class with Sami. It all helped. Gradually, I worked myself into a new routine, and when I was hit by a wave of sadness or loneliness, I reminded myself of all the wonderful things in my life, starting with my daughter, the baby I had on the way, the many special moments I had enjoyed with Charlie, and my precious, patient, strong, and supportive family.

As I got closer to delivering, I changed my mind about finding out the baby's sex, and I was ecstatic when my doctor said I was having another girl. Having grown up one of two girls, I loved the idea of sisters. I shared the news with Charlie. Obviously this pregnancy was a different experience from the first one, but I tried not to dwell on the negative. I kept moving forward. A baby was a blessing.

I moved out of our house and into a gated community where

I had more privacy and felt safer from the paparazzi, who'd stood outside our house every single day. They actually filmed over the fence. I felt too vulnerable there. But three days after moving, I encountered another unforeseen danger. During my checkup, my doctor saw that the cord was wrapped around the baby's neck. I wasn't at the point of delivering her right then, but nobody wanted it to get worse. An amnio was performed to see if her lungs were developed, and I was told to get ready just in case. Sure enough, the next afternoon I was instructed to return to the hospital, this time to have the baby.

I called Charlie, and he took me to the hospital. My mom came, too. I wanted her in the delivery room with me. Despite the fissure in our family unit, Lola was greeted upon her arrival on June 1, 2005, by an outpouring of love and affection. She was three weeks early, but seemed fine, weighing six pounds ten ounces. However, we had a brief scare. Moments after the nurse placed her on my chest, they snatched her away. She had stopped breathing and turned blue. They pumped fluid out of her and the fragile baby spent the night in the ICU.

I felt helpless seeing Lola with an IV in her tiny arm and needing oxygen to breathe. But she was my little fighter. By the next day, she was back with me, and three days later I took her home. Now I had two babies to raise on my own. Strangely, instead of being overwhelmed or scared, I felt the opposite—excited, blessed, and in a role meant for me.

Not that it was easy or perfect. I had one in diapers who was just learning to walk and a newborn that I was nursing every two to three hours. My mom was an invaluable stabilizing force at this crucial time, helping me with the girls, and also helping to settle us into the new house. She was never ruffled and preached the virtues of staying calm and dealing with life one dirty diaper at a time. Charlie's absence made me sad. As any new parent knows, countless special little moments happen with a newborn, as well as a one-year-old, and I missed not being able to share them with him.

Alas, as a newly separated mom I had a lot of issues to figure out. One issue that I had no questions about was Charlie's involvement with the girls. He spent Father's Day with us, and I wanted him present on every other family occasion. Even before I filed for divorce, I vowed our children were going to be raised by two parents. Divorced or not, I wanted the girls to grow up knowing how much we loved and cared for them.

3

TWO MONTHS AFTER Lola was born, I went back to work. *Sex, Love & Secrets* was picked up for thirteen episodes. Since I wasn't able to work out for six weeks again, I obviously hadn't lost all my pregnancy weight, but I shrugged off those concerns, figuring they'd shot me in the pilot while I was pregnant, they could no doubt figure out how to shoot around my postpregnancy figure. My boobs were big from nursing; that gave them something extra to focus on.

Bizarrely, I lost weight faster than after having Sami. I think it was because I could rest when Sami napped. With Lola, though, I was also busy taking care of a toddler. I rarely had time to close my eyes, let alone sit down for ten minutes. I'm sure the stress of the divorce also was a factor. One day when Lola was just a couple weeks old, my publicist called and said one of the glossy magazines had a photo of me coming out of a store. They wanted to know my tricks for losing my baby weight. "It's called divorce," I said with a rueful laugh.

Summer finally arrived. It's my favorite time of the year, and I got into a wonderful routine with the girls. I took Sami to the pool, entertained girlfriends, and had sleepovers with my sister, who was about to give birth to her third child. I also had special times with my mom, who stayed over on most weekends, if not more often, helping with the girls and talking with me for hours. We never ran out of conversation. I appreciated all the advice she had about raising children, as well as old family stories she shared, opportunities she gave me to ask her questions, and most of all just being a great listener as I tried to figure out my life.

She could tell that I obviously still loved Charlie, something I made no secret of. I wished our situation were different. Call me stubborn or stupid, but with the two girls, it was hard for me to accept it still couldn't be different.

Charlie seemed to think so, too. In August 2005, he began to spend time at my house and see the girls, and we started to talk. By early fall, Charlie suggested trying to repair our relationship, and when I asked what he had in mind, he said he wanted to work toward reconciliation.

Although being together as a family was what I wanted deep down, my reaction surprised me. I felt vulnerable. Yes, I was also excited, scared, and confused by the possibility of getting back together, but all the guilt I had about splitting up our family suddenly resurfaced—as did a myriad what-ifs that hinged on my decision. I don't believe two people should be together for the sake of children if their relationship is toxic, but Charlie and I seemed to be headed in the right direction, a sympathetic, open, and loving direction, and despite all my trepidations, I still loved him, and so I agreed we should give it another chance. I told my lawyer to put the divorce proceedings on hold while we attempted to figure some things out. I also slipped my wedding ring back on.

Deep down, I think I knew it wasn't going to work out. But I wanted to make sure we had done everything we could to make our family work. I didn't want any regrets.

So we went on a trip to the Caribbean to get away, be alone, and to try and save our marriage. In my heart of hearts, deep down, I was hoping that we would be able to make it work. But when some deep, dark revelations came to light and rocked me to my core, I knew it was best for my family and for me to get out for good.

I didn't, and still don't, regret seeing if we could rekindle our marriage. It was too important to not try, and I would've always wondered if I hadn't made the effort. However, as much as I wanted to save my marriage, as hard as I tried, it was done—and that finality was in some ways even harder than the first time we split. I went through all the same emotions again, plus more, and I moved forward with the divorce proceedings.

I knew God never gave a person more than he or she could

handle, and when I seemed to forget that, my mom reminded me. Her reassurances never wavered. Though I'm not one to complain or feel sorry for myself, I had no idea why I was being asked to handle what seemed like more than my fair share.

Little did I know how *much* more would come.

PART SEVEN

·

Relationships

1

....

IN MARCH 2006, I ran into Richie Sambora in a neighborhood restaurant parking lot, and from afar, our meeting looked like two acquaintances saying hello, which, I want to say emphatically, was exactly what happened. I didn't know Richie well, but we'd enjoyed each other's company on the handful of occasions he and his soon-to-be-ex, Heather Locklear, and Charlie and I had gone out to dinner. Both of us were going through difficult breakups with our spouses, and it felt as if we had a lot to say to each other. As for romantic sparks, as some in the press speculated, I can tell you there weren't any—then. We were in a parking lot. We said hi. Both Richie and I had a thousand things on our to-do lists other than starting another relationship at the same time we were trying to end marriages. In retrospect, of course, our chance encounter had all the elements of destiny— and disaster.

But before I get into what happened, why, and the effect it had on my life, I want to share my take on relationships and some of my romantic history, both of which will help shed light on my relationship with Richie. First, I've never been the kind of girl who has to have a boyfriend. I've never jumped from one relationship to the next. I know girls—and women—who do, some out of a fear of being alone, and others for different reasons. I've always been independent and would rather be single than be with the wrong partner.

My mom raised my sister and me to be able to take care of ourselves. She never wanted us to have to depend on a man. I guess that's partly why I've always been career-oriented and focused on being able to take care of myself financially. I always wanted to get married and have a family, but first I wanted to establish my career.

Not that I was ever anti-man. No way. I had some wonderful loves before I got married, and after. I've had great relationships with men, and I am still friendly with every ex-boyfriend. I have fond memories with all of them, and some not so fond, which is to be expected. But those have made me stronger and smarter. When a relationship ends, I don't see it as a failure. I believe there's always a reason we came together. I tell girlfriends that all the time. Look for the reason you were brought together. What did you enjoy? What did you learn?. It forces you to see something positive when you're going through the pain of a breakup, and later on, after the hurt fades, you have those better memories.

Before I was married, I believed we had only one soul mate in life. I credit my parents for that notion. They truly were soul mates. At the time of my divorce, they had been married more than thirty years and still held hands when they walked, still had date nights, and still were each other's best friend. After divorcing, I changed my tune. I didn't want to think that by my midthirties it was the end of my love life, that I'd never find a soul mate, and now I'm of the opinion that we have more than one soul mate and each special relationship is a beautiful journey with lessons to be learned.

If I sound romantic, it's because I am. I love being in love. I follow my heart even now after my difficult divorce.

Breakups can be incredibly painful, and the more in love, the harder the breakup. Looking back at my past relationships, they've taught me about men, about myself, and about life, and the lessons started early. I am thinking about my first serious relationship in high school—with James. We were your typical high school sweethearts. He was one grade ahead of me. We dated from my sophomore year until I was eighteen. He was a surfer, a hard-core surfer. I knew that at early morning and at dusk he was in the ocean. He even worked in a surf shop.

He was my first love, and when he graduated and I had a year left at high school without him, it was difficult being there. Away from school, we were together all the time. When I started to model, James often drove to L.A. with me for calls and photo shoots. During my first trip to Japan after graduation, we spoke as often as we could afford. At the beginning, our conversations lasted upward of two hours. Toward the end, they were two minutes. One time I called him and he answered, "Who's this?"

What the hell did he mean, "Who's this?" I was his girlfriend of three years! I had a sick feeling in my stomach after that call. I have good intuition, but I ignored it. We talked a few times after that, and before I flew home, I could hear him being distant. Something was up—or I should say something was evident beneath the surface. My roommate thought he was cheating on me. I thought she was crazy. There was no way James would cheat on me.

Standing next to my parents at the airport, he was all hugs and kisses welcoming me back home. He even gave me a bunch of little gifts. Later, my sister said he'd cheated on me the entire time I was gone, and I was devastated. I took those gifts to the surf shop where he worked and threw them in his face. That was the end of James.

He wanted to stay together, but there was no way in hell I could trust him again, and I didn't want to be with a guy who was going to cheat the minute I left town. But my anger quickly gave way to sadness, and I spent quite a few nights crying my eyeballs out. My dad came into my bedroom and tried to cheer me up. "I hate to tell you, this isn't going to be your only heart-ache," he said. "You'll have more."

If he was trying to make me feel better, he didn't. "I will never feel like this again," I argued. "I won't let it happen." Of course my father was right; he could've had a softer approach with me, but he was right on. In my twenties, I concentrated on my career, and I usually met guys when I was working on set or through my friends. I was a little naïve when I first moved to L.A. It was definitely a time of figuring things out, learning about the kind of man I was attracted to, learning about men in general, discovering the dynamics of dating and relationships, and preparing to find Mr. Right. Gradually, I began to develop a sense of the type of guy I wanted, the type of guy that made me happy, and the type of guy I wanted to please.

In my early twenties, I didn't have any responsibilities other than work, I could come and go as I pleased, and for the most part I wasn't too serious about anyone. It was all about hot guys and hot sex (and safe sex, I should add), dressing up, and having fun with nice people. As I matured, I discovered more about what I liked and needed. I realized I love a man, a real man, a guy's guy—someone who'll have my back and protect me, is loyal and kind, and makes me laugh.

I love a man who enjoys even the simple things, too, like staying up all night talking and eating ice cream in bed. And I insist on a great sexual connection, too, of course. You know Rihanna's song, "Only Girl"? That's how I want to feel with my man, that I'm the only girl—even if I'm not.

Aside from various boyfriends, and wonderful friends with a few benefits, I didn't get serious with anyone until I met Patrick Muldoon. I call him Pat. Actually, we call each other Shweetbabe. I know, it's silly, but to this day it's still Shweetbabe. As I said earlier, I met Pat in an acting class when I was nineteen, and we dated on and off for a few years while also dating other people. We didn't train our eyes solely on each other until we worked together on *Starship Troopers*, a six-month shoot where we got to know each other quite well, though it didn't happen easily.

That was the time everyone was reading the book *The Rules*. If they weren't reading it, they were talking about it. Such as my best friend, who kept telling me that I shouldn't be too interested in Pat. According to her, he had to pursue me, and the way to get him to do that was to play it cool. I was maybe too cool, which was dumb. Pat is gorgeous, and I hope he'll forgive me for being this honest, but he kind of knew it, which can be a good quality if a man plays that with a quiet confidence. And Pat did.

Girls threw themselves at him, and he handled them with an easy charm. In the meantime, I was so busy not throwing myself at him that he thought I didn't like him.

Not that he didn't try. He'd invite me out, but because he didn't ask me out on Wednesday for Saturday night, my girlfriend insisted I say I was busy. On Saturday, of course, I was home alone, wondering why I'd said I was busy. She also said I could only call him back after he called three times, but by the time I called him back, I was into that whole Wednesday-Saturday cycle. Seeing I was frustrated—I wonder why—she suggested I take a sexy dress to the set and get ready after we wrapped so Pat would see me leave all dressed up and think I had a hot date. I thought it was crazy, but I did it, and I felt like an ass leaving the set all dolled up only to meet my girlfriends for dinner.

I also went on a few dates with a guy—he called me early in the week so I was allowed to go—which pissed off Pat. In return, he brought a girl to the set, which, of course, angered me. All of a sudden we were pissed off at each other. Finally, I said screw *The Rules*, we talked, and everything came out. We told each other how we felt, and from then on Pat and I were officially together. And for the record, my girlfriend is *still* single.

To this day Pat is one of my best friends—and always will be. We went through too much together, from the early days of our relationship when no one knew either of us, through the making of *Wild Things*, whose risqué scenes were rough on Pat and caused a few fights, which we survived. But the Bond movie took a toll on us. Even though he made many trips to see me, and I flew home when I could, six months in London was a long time to be away from home. When the picture wrapped, we were still together—but barely.

Pat had a slight jealous side to him, and it was difficult for him when other men paid attention to me. One time we were at a premiere for one of his movies, and a guy was too forward with me. He grabbed my ass and Pat put his fist into the guy's head. The bouncer nearly booted him from his own party. In the end, the ass grabber was the one who got tossed onto the sidewalk, and everything worked out—except us.

My visibility and newfound fame as a "sex symbol" put a strain on our relationship. For me, it was my job. I was able to separate the two. Pat had a difficult time. To appease him, I found myself downplaying exciting things going on in my career. I wanted Pat to know how much I loved him and how much he meant to me. Ultimately we broke up, and it was one of my hardest breakups.

Actually, it wasn't a clean break. We got back together, broke up, and went back and forth like that for a while. Then I met Charlie.

2

AFTER CHARLIE, MY perspective on relationships was no longer the same as when I was in my twenties. I would've been in trouble if it had been. I'd been married, divorced, had two children, and I was in my thirties. I was in a different place compared to where I was when I'd met Charlie. I had major responsibilities, and before I considered my needs, I thought about my children, and the big picture, which you do as a parent, and that caused the little, petty crap that might've bothered me ten years earlier to not matter as much, if at all.

Richie understood the challenges and priorities of being a single parent. He was married to Heather Locklear and they have one daughter. And to clarify, yes, I was friendly with his ex, but only for a brief time, and my friendship with her had ended prior to anything that happened between Richie and me. That's the truth. I did not break up a marriage. It was already over. Had she and I still been friends, I never would have crossed that line with him. Ever.

My relationship with Richie happened when I least expected it, though running into him may have been inevitable. In fact, I'm surprised it hadn't happened before. He lived two minutes from me. During our conversation in the parking lot, I found out he was home while on break from Bon Jovi's latest tour, and with both of us going through divorces, we decided to catch up, and we traded phone numbers.

Soon we talked on the phone. Not surprisingly, we shared a lot of common experiences and concerns. Among other things, we were going through divorces, we knew each other's spouses, we worried about our children, we came from tight families with parents who'd been married forever, and we had stories about going through a divorce. Then there was the everyday stuff. Quite simply, it was a relief to speak openly about everything and know it would stay between the two of us.

After that first conversation, we were dialing each other daily, if not several times a day. In all the time I knew Richie when we were both married, I never looked at him in a romantic way. I was married and in love with my husband. No one was more surprised than I was when I began to think about him in a different way. There was nothing wrong with that, I told myself. We were both single. He was smart, funny, sensitive, and sympathetic. I knew he was starting to have strong feelings for me, too—and this was just over the phone. It was a dilemma, and for many reasons I wished those feelings hadn't been there.

But they were real, and when Richie suggested getting together in person, I had to make a complicated decision. It was either move forward with this friendship or stop talking to him altogether. There was no in-between. My heart told me to see him, but my head said to run in the other direction. Deep down, I already knew what I was going to do. The problem was avoiding the paparazzi that followed me every day as soon as I ventured beyond my gate.

But Richie and I hatched a plan. I snuck out late at night; my SUV had dark-tinted windows, making it nearly impossible for any photographers to get a shot if they were still waiting outside my gate at that hour. Then, for me to get through his gate without the guard seeing me, Richie waited in his car outside his gate and I followed him in without stopping to give my name. It worked.

Our visit, which followed weeks of conversations on the phone and anticipation of this get-together, was magical. We did nothing but talk for five hours. I left after that and we arranged to get together a few days later. We talked on the phone several times a day. We had code names for each other. I was Lucy, and he was Jack. If I didn't answer my phone, he'd say it was Jack calling for Denise. Jack also sent flowers. And Lucy did the same when Jack was back on tour. Under this veil of playful but necessary secrecy, our romance blossomed.

Richie and I shared an easiness I hadn't before had. We were able to be open, honest, and completely authentic with each other, with no judgment. It was refreshing to not have to hide any aspect of myself, or to pretend. I felt as if I were taking my first breaths of fresh air in ages. But there was a slight problem with our being together. Given the circumstances with his soon-to-be-ex-wife, I knew that news of our relationship was not going to play well. It was dangerous territory.

I agonized about the situation and potential fallout. Technically we weren't doing anything wrong. We were both single, getting divorced. I couldn't deny how I felt about him and how he made me feel, and he felt the same way.

Whenever Richie had a break from Bon Jovi's tour, he flew back to L.A. and we rendezvoused at one of our houses. He still waited outside the gate for me at his place, though slowly we got brave enough to where I went through his gate without an escort. One time I drove to his gate and the guard said, "Hi, Denise." I said hello and explained I was going to Richie's. "But I don't have you down here," he said, checking his list. "All I have is Lucy."

That was odd. Every other time I'd come over, Richie had cleared my name. Slightly flustered, I stupidly said Lucy was in the backseat of my car, thinking he'd let me go through. But, nope, he asked if I could roll down the window so he could see her. At that point, I was dying. "You can't really see her," I said. "She's tiny." He wouldn't let up. He craned his neck to try to see around me and into the backseat. Finally, with my face red and sweaty, I blurted out, "I'm Lucy!" With a complicit nod, he said, "Oh," and opened the gate.

It was funny—but just the start of complications.

3

AT THIS POINT, only a few close friends, family members, and the guards at our respective gates knew about our relationship. One day Charlie was visiting the girls (they were babies at this point) at my house when Richie called. My housekeeper answered and came into the room. In front of Charlie, she said Richie was on the phone. He'd forgotten to say Jack. Charlie's eyes widened; he wasn't stupid.

But it turned out fine. As we continued forward through the minefield of our breakup, Charlie began a relationship with Brooke Mueller. I was happy for him and made it a priority to develop a good rapport with her. I advise women whose exes get involved with other women to do the same: establish a friendship. Life is calmest when everyone gets along.

When Charlie got serious with Brooke, I wanted to meet her. Whether I liked Brooke or not, which I did, or still had issues with Charlie, was beside the point. For me, it was all about doing what was best for my children. When they came home one day and told me she had given them candy when Daddy didn't know,

I wasn't mad. I understood she was trying to bond with my girls. She wanted them to like her.

The next time our nanny brought the girls to Charlie's, I gave her a package for Brooke with a bunch of girly stuff I knew Sam and Lola liked, including makeup and dress-up items—stuff she could do with the girls. I also enclosed a note telling Brooke that I looked forward to meeting her and was glad Charlie was happy.

I meant every word. I didn't feel threatened that this woman was going to play with my girls. Nor did I worry whether they'd like her, which they did. I wanted Sam and Lola to be surrounded by love. Sure, it was odd at first. But that was normal and it lessened over time. That November I hosted everyone at Thanksgiving dinner. Charlie brought Brooke, Richie was my date, my parents were there, and my sister and her family filled out the rest of the table.

Talk about an interesting evening. But it was the best thing for Sam and Lola to see us all getting along and enjoying a wonderful "family" holiday together. Of course, everyone talked privately after dinner. Don't all families? But the children had a great time, gave hugs and kisses afterward, and went to bed to a chorus of "I love you."

I kept inviting Charlie for dinner, and he came. If we had a conflict, I told him to "put our shit aside, turn that frown upside down, and whistle 'Dixie' out your ass if you have to. I don't care if you hate me, but fake it in front of the kids. We need to present a mom and dad who can be friendly with each other, which will give them a sense of security." Sometimes it worked. Other times it didn't go so well. At least I tried.

Alone, I had my share of anger, hurt, and frustration. I vented to my parents and trusted girlfriends, but for one dinner or a Sunday brunch I could suck it up.

Despite those efforts, though, we had our ups and downs, and our divorce turned hostile. Then it got worse; it got toxic. Charlie and I have extremely different views about the way children should be raised and the kind of environment that's healthy for them. I wanted my girls to have a great relationship with their dad, but during times that I didn't think were appropriate for two young, impressionable girls, it was my job as their mom to be protective. He disagreed.

It's public knowledge that I filed for a restraining order, but what's not known is that two previous times I tried to handle things privately.

But by spring 2006, things hadn't changed and it had gotten so bad I couldn't take it anymore and I filed with the court. That was a very scary time for me because I was told that if I filed with the court, the records wouldn't be sealed, but I felt like I had no choice. And that's when everything exploded. From that day on, my life was never the same.

I needed to get away from the stress and the hostility. So, Richie and I decided to go someplace where it would be just the two of us and I wouldn't have to worry about Charlie, lawyers, paparazzi . . . anything.

Richie had a beach house in Laguna. We picked a weekend when my parents could stay with my daughters. He went directly there, and I snuck down on my own. At least I thought I did. Somehow the paparazzi found us. To this day I don't know if they followed me or were tipped off or both. They ended up staking out Richie's house from a quarter of a mile away, in the ocean (someone at a magazine relayed that info to us later). With their long, powerful lenses trained on Richie's house and the beach, they snapped us on his private balcony. We had no idea.

Driving home, I got a phone call from my publicist, a call that to this day makes me ill. She told me about the pictures. She said she was being inundated with calls from media outlets. Everyone had questions about Richie and me. It was big news.

My heart sank.

I got sick to my stomach.

By the time I got past my front door, I was in a daze. I didn't know what to think or how to feel; I was just numb. Later, as I calmed down, I was mortified. We got caught in the worst way. I was so humiliated by the way our relationship was exposed.

If you didn't know the truth about Richie and me, which few did, it had the scent of scandal, and I knew the press would spin it in that direction. I braced myself for the onslaught. It wasn't going to be pretty, but I thought, "Okay, I can deal with a week of shitty press."

If only it had been a week. My entire world came crashing down overnight. It was the worst time of my life (this was before my mom got sick). The press about our relationship was horrendous and lasted not weeks or months, but a couple of years. No exaggeration. Until then, I'd always been presented in a positive light, as a nice person, the good girl, if you will. Even coverage of my divorce painted me in an empathetic light. But that changed in a day, literally overnight. Suddenly I was a home wrecker and a husband stealer, Hollywood's latest villainess. Few knew the truth, but the truth didn't seem to matter. I was hurt, humiliated, and embarrassed. It felt as if everyone in the world hated me, and I believed they did.

Ironically, prior to this episode, one of my agents had joked that I needed more edge. "There are too many pictures of you pushing a stroller," he said, laughing. "Can't you get arrested or something?" I'd warned him to be careful what he wished for, which he reminded me of when all this shit came raining down on me. "I wish you'd gotten arrested instead," he said. It was that bad.

But there were a few bright spots. Sam gave me wonderful hugs and kisses, and Lola learned to crawl. And then there was Richie. His smile brightened the darkest days. If there was anything positive about the whole world knowing we were involved, it was the freedom it gave us to live our lives out in the open. We went to restaurants and lingered over lunch. We held hands as we got coffee. He drove me to the store when I needed to pick up diapers. We were like a normal couple except that the paparazzi constantly took pictures of us while shouting questions and comments, trying to elicit a reaction that would make their photos more valuable.

But it only strengthened our bond, and personally, it made me one strong bitch. I realized I was tough as nails, and able to handle way more than I'd realized, and though it's taken me a long time to come to terms with living like that, the lessons I learned were a blessing in disguise. But I wouldn't figure that out for some time.

Richie went back on the road and asked me to meet him in

Europe. At first, I hesitated. I'd done a pilot that didn't get picked up, and with all the rotten press I was getting, I didn't know if it was worth giving the world more ammunition to speculate and criticize. My mom urged me to ignore the critics and gossips. "Don't worry about anyone else," she said. "Live your life as best you can while you can." I knew where those words of hers came from, and she was right, of course. Richie wanted me with him, and I needed to escape and have fun, and I was able to leave the girls with my parents, who adored having the little ones to themselves.

I met Richie in Dublin, Ireland, and watched Bon Jovi's show from the side of the stage. After the gig, we flew to Naples in the middle of the night, hoping the press wouldn't find us. We drove along the magnificent Amalfi Coast to our hotel in Positano, Italy. Somehow the press found us, photos surfaced, and we were accused of flaunting our relationship. We weren't. We just wanted to live our lives. We didn't want to keep hiding. It felt good to be with him, and to this day, I have never laughed more than I have with him.

In May, I was back in L.A. and trying to establish some routine in my life when I received some devastating news: my mom's cancer had returned. My dad called; my mom was too upset to even talk, which in itself communicated the gravity of the situation. I lost it, and I don't know what I would've done without Richie, who assured me that he'd help my mom and me in any way he could.

Two weeks later, Richie called me with tragic news of his own. His father had just been diagnosed with lung cancer. It was unbelievable. What were the odds? Here we were, both going through difficult divorces, both struggling with single parent-hood, and now our parents had cancer. It's often hard to con-template the workings of fate, but this wasn't one of those times. I saw why Richie and I had been brought together. It made so much sense. As we went through this incredibly difficult phase of our lives, we had each other, and we understood each other as only we could.

A strong, solid relationship would've had difficulty weather-ing such a challenging time. Ours was still fairly new, and sadly, I supposed, it was inevitable that these enormous challenges would start to take a toll on our relationship. But we stayed to-gether. Like glue. When Richie's dad lost his battle with lung cancer, I was with him at the hospital in New York. It was ter-ribly sad and only made me more concerned and fearful of my situation at home, where my mom continued her brave fight.

Not long after, Richie and I broke up. The stress was finally too much to shoulder. My divorce was especially heated and contentious, and Richie was dealing with other things on his end. Ending the relationship was sad and hard; he was a dear friend with whom I had some wonderful times and confided some of my darkest fears, and it was hard to give that up. But I needed to focus on my divorce, which had unfortunately turned into a messy custody issue, and my career, which the negative press had affected badly.

I was left with mixed emotions. I paid a dear price for my relationship with Richie, and I'd be lying if I said I've never wondered how things might've been different if I hadn't got in-volved with him. I know I harp on the press I got at that time, but for good reason: it was almost unbearable. I do understand why it was perceived the way it was, and looking back, perhaps I should've handled it differently. But I don't regret my relationship with him. I learned hard lessons from our journey together. My heart may have been bruised, but it was pure. Richie is a wonderful man. He came into my life when I needed him, and he needed me. We'll always have that bond.

The lessons I learned from my relationship with Richie, especially from the fallout in the media, changed the way I think and act and relate to other people. Before, I was careful with my image and basically a people pleaser, someone who tried to say what I thought was expected rather than what was true. Since then, I've lived my life the way I choose to live it; I make choices for me and my kids. What you see is what you get. I'm fine knowing that not everyone is going to like me. That's life. I'm being my authentic self, and something about that is freeing.

A little secret: Richie and I saw each other a few times in the years after we broke up. No one knew it because we reverted back to our original tricks. We called us "The Jack and Lucy Show." We never went out in public. One night, after the girls went to bed, he came to my house. We were talking in my room (thank goodness that's all we were doing) when I heard Sami at my door. I motioned for Richie to hide in my bathroom. It turned out Sami's tummy hurt. I had her lie on my bed and told Richie to give me a few minutes while I calmed her down and got her back to her own bed. On the way back to her room, she threw up, which triggered my phobia. I couldn't believe it. Nor could I rush her back into my bathroom. Richie was stuck in there.

I ran back to tell him what was going on. I don't freak out

easily, but I was a wreck. Knowing I had a hard time with throw-up, he offered to help. But I didn't want Sam to see him. As I cleaned her up, she puked again. I woke up my housekeeper, who helped, while I told Richie he had to crawl the fuck out of my room. He shook his head, he thought I was nuts! At six feet two inches, he wasn't going to crawl, which would've been kind of funny. "In that case, you're going to be in the bathroom a while," I said.

Such are the complications of having a social life as a single parent. My girls, though close to Richie when we dated, hadn't seen him since our breakup. I didn't want to confuse them. That's why I didn't want Sami to see him, especially when the poor thing was so sick. I don't know if that's right or wrong. It's just my way. I get advice from friends, but mostly I go with my gut. Dating as a single mom is difficult. Period. I want a dating life, but I also don't want my kids to see me with a bunch of different men. Nor do I want the media turning a first date at a coffee shop into a hot new relationship. I do the best I can to let acquaintances develop naturally into friendships and perhaps more. To ensure privacy, I've had dates in hotel rooms and then gone home after dessert. It's not about hanky-panky; it's about trying to balance dating as a single mom discreetly.

Being aware of the differences in dating and relationships at this time in my life helps me get over the hurdles. First, I've realized life is too short not to compromise. If there's conflict, I like to resolve it and move on. I don't harp on the past. I had a friend who was pissed her husband went to a strip club, and she was still bringing it up seven years later. Don't waste the energy. Drop it and move forward—or examine what the real problem is. In addition, I don't try to change a man. Not only is it impossible, why would I want to? Actually, the better question is this: what would I be doing with a man I wanted to change?

Take cigarettes. Charlie chain-smoked. I tried my first puff on our honeymoon and nearly choked to death. That one puff was more than enough for me. But I didn't bug Charlie to quit, and I wouldn't do it if I was with another guy that smoked. It's not fair to him. If you're fine with it in the beginning, you better be fine with it two years later. If you date a guy who drinks his face off and think he's going to quit after you get married, you're going to be disappointed, because he'll probably end up drinking even more after you get married. In my marriage, I discovered things about Charlie that I didn't know beforehand, and those were the crux of our problems. I didn't give him a hard time about the things I was aware of during our relationship.

Experience along with age has made me more tolerant and practical. I no longer play hard to get, the way I did in my twenties (not that I'd advise anyone to use those tactics). I'm an open book. If I like someone, I let him know it, and if he likes me, I lay out the facts of my life ahead of time so he knows exactly what he's getting into.

As a single, working mom, my time is precious. I don't wait for a man to call three times before I call back. I'm spontaneous. If someone I like calls Saturday morning to go out that night, and I'm free, I'll say yes. Sometimes I need more time to plan. It depends. Years ago, I checked my voice mail every fifteen minutes. Now, I'm lucky if I check it once a week. I've realized there are no rules. I let my heart and common sense guide me through the straits and narrows of amour.

Dating experts may not agree, but these methods work for me, though what am I really talking about? Honesty. Openness. And communication. It's that simple. If it's too much for a guy, then it's not meant to be, and I'm okay with that.

I do still have my insecurities with dating. At times I wonder, who the hell would want to jump into this chaos with me? Even though Charlie and I have been divorced for six years, he is very much a part of my life and forever will be. My baggage is the size of a fucking U-Haul, and it's going to take a strong, secure man to be in a relationship with me. The good part? He will have a house full of girls who will adore him. I find myself now being more attracted to men with children. Seeing a man who is a good dad? There is nothing sexier! Remember that picture of Brad Pitt with the baby bottle in his back pocket? Now that's a man, and a sexy father, I might add!

One other tip: I never tell my girls I'm going on a date. When they ask where I'm going, I say that I have a meeting. Technically, I'm not lying. And my gut tells me to keep calling these "meetings" until I meet my next Mr. Right.

PART EIGHT

·

Loss

1

....

AS YOU CAN tell, I'm a big proponent of living in the moment. To not focus so much on the past and to try not to worry about the future. We never know what's going to happen or what kind of cards we're always going to be dealt. I learned to truly enjoy the simplest things in life. When I felt as if I were drowning, I dug deep in my soul to remember what was important. I have two gorgeous, healthy children, a beautiful home; I'm healthy and happy, and I have wonderful friends and family who give me love and support. I reminded myself that I did have my feet firmly planted on the ground despite what was being written about me. My daughters made an out-of-control situation more manageable.

I try to embrace the good moments and savor every morsel. Watching Lola learn to crawl was a joyous event amid a dismal time, as well as a reminder that life goes on no matter what, and I was very conscious of paying attention and appreciating that milestone. We can choose whether we get on with life or root ourselves in the past. My approach is to deal and move on. To enjoy every moment. I know it's basic pop psychology, but it works for me.

One of the most special moments of my whole life was in

May. My mom drove up for a visit, and while she was at the house, we did a photo shoot for a special Mother's Day album in *People* magazine. We represented three generations—my mom, me, and Sam and Lola. We had a lovely day, and I treasured those photos then and even more now. They are the last pictures I have of all of us before my mom started to look ill.

A week later, my dad called with the news her cancer had returned. My mind was reeling with thoughts after I hung up, including the afternoon we spent posing for pictures. It stood out like a breezy Saturday in my childhood, a perfect day I wished could last forever. The Polaroids from the shoot were still on my kitchen counter. How did that day suddenly seem so long ago?

Life changed that fast. I've never been one to feel sorry for myself or ask, why me? No matter what I was going through, no matter the challenges or frustrations I faced, I knew my life was blessed. I have two healthy children, my bills are paid, and no matter what, I'd tell myself it could always be worse. Well, this was worse. As far as I was concerned, it was *the* worst thing I could imagine. I found myself asking, why her? Why was this happening to my mom?

She never asked that question herself. No, she was the one who, when we finally talked, tried to comfort me by saying, "It could be worse. It could've been one of the kids." That attitude had gotten her through the first bout of cancer nearly two years earlier. I replayed that time in my head as if I could will another outcome. For about six months prior to diagnosis, she'd been slowed by shoulder pain, calcium deposits, headaches, a constant ache in her right side, and forgetfulness, which wasn't at all like my mom, who was razor sharp and on top of everything.

Her doctor had attributed it to premenopausal aches and pains. That never sounded right to me, but no tests were ever ordered.

She and my dad flew to Chicago to visit their best friends, Diane and Tom. By the time their plane landed, though, my mom was doubled over in pain. Diane's daughter was a nurse, and they rushed my mom to the hospital where she worked. The ER doctor who examined my mom helped her with the pain but told her she needed to get an MRI when she got home. He knew what was wrong but didn't tell her. At home, she found out the story: renal cell carcinoma—or kidney cancer.

A smoker, she gave up cigarettes that day. She was pissed at how easily she quit after numerous failed attempts over the years. It shows you the power of the mind. She also sent the ER doctor in Chicago a note thanking him for what she thought was his saving her life. At her diagnosis, she'd been told her cancer was stage 2, still early enough to give her a fighting chance, though there wasn't treatment for kidney cancer at the time. Chemo and radiation were ineffective. They had to remove her kidney, then pray it didn't come back.

I was making *Elvis Has Left the Building* in Santa Fe when she went in for surgery. I left the set and flew directly to San Diego. She was already in surgery when I arrived. I waited with my dad until they wheeled my mom into her room from surgery. The sight of her in bed connected to all the tubes and still suffering extreme pain scared the shit out of me, yet I put on a brave face. When she opened her eyes, I wanted her to see me staring back with love, strength, support, and hope—all the same things she'd been giving me.

Her spirits rose when she heard I was having another little girl, but the good news was tempered by a distressing report. Her surgeons found her cancer had spread and was stage 4, not stage 2 as originally thought. The odds had already been bad; now they were worse. But my mom was a fighter. She loved life and loved being a grandma. If anyone could beat the disease, it was my mom, and she came out of the surgery with the right attitude, vowing to do whatever it took.

For a while, it looked as if she might be one of the lucky few. She was cancer-free as my marriage to Charlie dissolved and I took up with Richie. In between CAT scans, which she had every three months, she provided me comfort and encouragement. When I was going through my divorce and everything else, my mom was my rock through it all. "You're so much stronger than you think," she said. I would tell her I felt guilty, even telling her about my challenges when here she was facing the biggest challenge of her life. But, she explained, "I'm your mother. Cancer doesn't stop that." After her cancer returned, she put on a brave face despite fearing what lay ahead. In that alone, she presented a powerful and lasting lesson that I return to daily. Facing the worst, my mom showed me how to be my best.

2

....

DURING A BREAK from Bon Jovi's European tour, Richie flew home and we arranged for our cancer-stricken parents to undergo exams at the famed MD Anderson Cancer Center in

Houston. All of us—Richie's parents and my parents and the two of us—flew there and met with a team of specialists. Earlier, my mom had done a few days of experimental chemo and gotten so sick she had to be hospitalized. It nearly killed her. So we were desperate to find another option for her and the best available treatment for Richie's dad.

We spent part of a week there. During the day, Richie and I went with our parents to their appointments and then spent the nights going out to wonderful dinners in an effort to lighten the mood. Not surprisingly, none of us had much of an appetite. During one of my mom's appointments, she broke down, and it broke my heart. She couldn't help herself. The doctors were extremely frank about the severity of her condition and the difficulty of treatment. They were kind and human, but direct, and their directness carried a frightening gravity. It was like driving straight into the concrete wall of mortality.

I did everything I could to stay strong for her. The doctors at Anderson set up a treatment plan for her with a new specialist close to home. There wasn't much to do except try another drug, a new kind of chemo taken orally, which we thought wouldn't cause the same severe side effects as the previous chemo she'd tried. But we were wrong. I don't know how my mom battled that horrific disease, but she did. It was sheer force of will—the will to live. The *People* magazine with our Mother's Day picture came out and I would stare at the original in my living room, the four of us, with my mom still looking healthy, her eyes dancing with brightness as she cuddled with her granddaughters, and I'd think, why her? Even if it was her, why couldn't she beat it? Why was the disease unrelenting, uncaring, and unloving?

That summer, I moved into a slightly bigger home to have enough room for my parents to stay over when they could, which wasn't often enough. My mom's new chemo drug made her very sick. I made sure to visit every weekend that she was feeling up to it. I was also distracted much of the time by my custody fight with Charlie. Communication between us dwindled to nil, and the tone, at least on his end, was nasty. When I dropped the kids off for his visitation, I wasn't allowed inside the gate of his community. I had to sit in my car until someone from his house drove out and got my nanny and the girls. I hated to leave them. It broke my heart. A similar routine took place when I arrived to pick them up. One time a handyman brought them back out. It confused the kids. It was awful. I cried every time I drove away after dropping them off. I'd ask myself, "How did this happen? How'd we get to this point?" I had no choice; that's what was in our stipulation.

Our custody case required what seemed like endless depositions and court visits. It also devastated me to sit across from the man I married, the man I thought I'd be with forever, and have him glare at me for seven hours while I was questioned about the most intimate details of my—no, *our* life. I felt exposed in so many ways, though I got to the point where I didn't care what I was asked or what name I was called as long as I protected the girls.

There was endless speculation in the media about our battle. I was called a gold digger, vindictive, and crazy. It wasn't easy to be pitted against the star of America's favorite sitcom—something he reminded me about constantly. I felt at times I was fighting a losing battle. Everyone loved Charlie and thought I was the evil wife who stole her best friend's husband. I felt that I was misjudged before anyone else had any facts. I never wanted our personal business to be public. At one desperate low point when I almost let loose, a friend said, "Remember, you're a mom first. The other stuff doesn't matter." My mom, a constant support, kept me focused and strong. She wrapped her arms around me and said, "It may not seem like it now, but you'll get through it—and the truth will come out."

For Charlie, it was about the fight. He said he would bleed me dry financially and swore I'd never win. He vowed to destroy me, and I have to say, it often felt as if he was going to succeed. I also wondered why he felt the need to show up in court with his publicist.

My savings disappeared. My legal fees got so high I almost had to relent. My parents offered to sell their house to help pay the bills. People have since heard the way Charlie has exploded on his *Two and a Half Men* bosses in interviews. As you may imagine, I have been on the other end of that voice many times—I've experienced it in person and seen it in print. And it ain't pretty. I felt maligned and misunderstood. So many times I wanted to publicly defend myself. The few times I did, I actually made things worse. So I stopped. But my girls held me up. I'd see them at the dinner table or check on them at night as they slept and feel a surge of strength where I had none before.

Finally, I told Charlie to stop holding press conferences. If he had an issue with me, he should file it with the court. We had a short window with the girls before they'd catch on to the insanity, and I wanted to preserve every moment of innocence they had. It was surreal to have breakfast with my daughters, and then off I went to battle their dad in court. They would see me dressed up and wonder where I was going. I always told them I had an important meeting.

I remember sort of joking with my lawyer that I'd run out of conservative outfits to wear to court, telling him, "We have to wrap this up." My mother was battling for her life, and I didn't want to continue fitting in phone calls and visits between court appearances. I drove to Encinitas as frequently as possible. My mom's treatments made her sick, and the days she was really ill, we stayed home because she didn't want us to see her that way. But when she had a good day, we would head down to visit her. I cried every time we drove away. I saw her body changing drastically. My dad turned into her full-time caretaker. Before she got sick, she did all the cooking and cleaning. Now my dad had to learn how to cook. Plus he cleaned the house, managed doctor appointments, treatments, and kept track of all her medications—a complex task, as anyone who has been in a similar situation knows. He had a schedule and a huge pillbox to keep it all organized and make sure she got all her meds.

My mom's biggest fear was that the cancer would spread to her brain and her bones, and in an effort to prevent that terrible turn, she was willing to tolerate any and all discomfort without complaint. In that respect, she was remarkable, almost saintlike.

If only I'd had her grace during an incident while shooting the movie *Blonde and Blonder* in Vancouver. One day, as I worked on a scene with Pamela Anderson, one of the paparazzi crossed the line with me and I lost my temper, which is unusual for me. Even under the most trying circumstances, I rarely blow up. I go the other way; I withdraw. But not this time. He wouldn't leave Pam and me alone. (You have to understand that some of these guys ask rude and aggressive questions as they shoot, hoping to provoke you into lashing back and giving them something juicy to sell. This guy was one of those.) I offered to give him some shots if he'd let us work. He responded with an outburst of vulgarity and insults not only directed at me but at my family.

Well, even though I knew better, I lost it. I picked up his laptop and hurled it over the balcony. I'd never done anything remotely like that in my life. He just pushed the wrong button at the wrong time. It was just built-up crap of all the negative stories week after week, my mom was so sick, we were working sixteen-to-eighteen-hour days, and I was traveling back and forth between L.A. and Vancouver as frequently as possible, and after this guy insulted my family, I let loose. Granted he was being a prick, but I could've handled the situation differently. I had a couple lawsuits from that incident so there were definitely consequences for my actions, and I dealt with it. Now, I am nice to all the paparazzi.

That unfortunate incident was followed by good news. After I wrapped the movie, we got word that my mom's tumors had all shrunk significantly, to where they were close to nothing. We were ecstatic. We took that as a major reprieve from immediate danger. It seemed there was a payoff to all the discomfort she'd endured. She had to keep having her scans every couple of months, but the new drug had worked.

Anyone who has dealt with cancer knows it's a roller coaster of hopes, dreams, fears, and countless other emotions, and we were finally in a good spot.

3

....

IN FEBRUARY OF 2007 my mom decided to get a tattoo. It was, she later explained, something she'd always wanted to do. But she didn't tell any of us at the time, not even my dad. Her best friend, Diane, was in town, visiting, and the two of them went to a tattoo parlor my brother-in-law, Brandon (he's covered head to toe), recommended. The tattoo artist there, one of Brandon's friends, promised to do a great job on my mom. Brandon didn't even tell my sister.

At the tattoo parlor, my mom was about to get inked when she had a seizure. The poor guy who was getting set to work on her didn't know what to do. Diane stepped in, helped my mom, told the guy to call an ambulance and then to call Brandon, who, in turn, phoned my sister, who called my dad. Although no one called me, I had a premonition that something had happened to my mom. I don't claim to be psychic, but I might as well have been standing next to an alarm as it went off. I knew from the sinking feeling in my gut there was a problem.

I tried repeatedly to get ahold of my dad, but his cell went directly to voice mail. Finally, Diane called me as my mom was on her way to the emergency room. I grabbed Richie, who was sitting next to me in my office. A few minutes later, my dad called from the hospital. He confirmed the worst. My mom's cancer had spread to her brain.

I could barely move. I felt my heart sink and take me down with it. Richie got us a car and we went straight to the hospital.

I could barely speak the whole drive there. I knew this was the beginning of the end, which I didn't want to even think about. A recurrence was bad enough. Once the cancer spreads to the brain, though, the chances of recovery are slim to impossible, and the side effects—the only thing my mom feared—can make it all the worse.

She definitely wasn't herself when I saw her at the hospital. She was giddy and animated, in an almost childlike manner, and kind of out of it, all of which the doctor said was due to the seizure. Seeing her like that frightened me. I kissed her face, touched my hand to her cheek, rubbed her shoulder, and glanced at my dad with a look conveying questions and concern. I wondered if she'd ever be herself again.

Once the effects of the seizure wore off, she did become herself again, but with another long, scary, uncertain road ahead of her. The doctor shared the horrible news with us: not only had the cancer spread, she had forty tumors in her brain. Forty! How the hell was that possible? I didn't understand. We were told the tumors in her body had shrunk, and yet her brain was now full of them. Again, how the hell was that possible?

I was so pissed, angry, confused. I was convinced the chemo had killed the tumors in her body but in some way caused the cancer to spread to her brain. My theory was unfounded, but I didn't know how else she could go within a few months from having a clear brain to having forty tumors there. I didn't get it. I was crushed. So was my dad, who hung his head in defeat, trying to hide his tears.

My mom never gave up hope and infused us with her beautiful spirit and will to continue living. "I'm not giving up," she said, taking each of our hands in hers. "I don't plan on losing this fight. Thanks to all of you, I have too much to live for."

She started radiation on her brain. Though she lost her hair after the second treatment, her body seemed able to tolerate it. After the first couple of weeks, though, it made her sick. Unfortunately, my custody battle veered into uglier and more challenging territory. Many days I was tied up in depositions lasting upward of seven hours. I didn't understand Charlie's hostility, and I resented him for getting me riled up to where I fought back. My only intention was to do what was best for our daughters. We needed to keep the focus on them, I argued, not the two of us. It was surreal to sit across from the man I once loved with all my heart as he glared at me as if I were the enemy while our attorneys took turns asking us the most intimate details about our marriage. They also brought in people who had worked for us.

It was a disturbing, debilitating, and demeaning exercise in anger. It took me away from caring for the children. It took me away from spending time with my mom as she battled a terrible disease. What was the point?

I left one deposition on the verge of a panic attack and had to pull off the freeway until I calmed down. Between the fighting in court, the leaks that ended up in the press, the toll it was taking on my career (offers and auditions dried up), and worry about my mom, I was constantly on overload. Only seeing the girls at home allowed me to maintain perspective no matter what kind of day I had.

Even that was put to the test when Richie called from the road and told me his father had taken a sudden turn. He was in the hospital and expected to pass away that night. Getting on the first available plane, I met Richie at the hospital in New York. His dad made it through the night and held on for the next week. We were at the hospital every day until he finally ran out of fight and died peacefully surrounded by those who loved him. My heart broke for Richie and his mom.

Watching them deal with their grief while planning the wake and funeral made me distraught and anxious about my mom's plight. I stole away to a quiet corner of the house and called her doctor. Explaining that my boyfriend had just lost his father, I asked about my mom's prognosis. "I need to know the truth," I said.

According to the doctor, a new drug was on the verge of being approved for testing and my mom would be a candidate for it. I asked a few follow-up questions about the drug, then found myself telling the doctor about my mom, who was only fifty-three and looking forward to my sister giving birth to her third child soon. "She'll have five grandchildren," I said. "She has so much to live for." The doctor understood. "I adore your mom," she said. "She has a wonderful spirit."

Richie came into the room and handed me a tissue. Tears were flowing down my face. I thought about my mom still bravely going through her radiation treatments and taking steroids to control the swelling in her brain that caused headaches so intensely painful that she dropped to her knees to weather them. Would the experimental drug, if it even became available in time, make a difference? I mustered my courage. "What I really want to know is how long she has," I said. "With or without the drug, how long does she have to live? Does she even have a chance? From your experience, can you give me an estimate?"

The doctor paused. "If your mom is in a coma tomorrow, I wouldn't be surprised; if it is six months from now, I won't be surprised, either."

She had up to six months left to live.

4

....

BACK IN L.A., I made sure the time my mom had left was filled with family and love. I never told my sister or my dad about my conversation with the doctor, and of course I never said anything to my mom. She never asked that question of her doctor. Likewise, she never once gave up hope. Nor did she give up her role as mom, grandma, and chief supporter, cheerleader, and rock of the family. She nurtured me when I ended my relationship with Richie, understanding that we'd helped each other through extraordinary times in our lives, but because we handled pain and stress differently, it was best to part ways, though it didn't mean we wouldn't be there for each other in times of need.

I focused on my mom and children. Despite being sick and weak, my mom came up for Lola's second birthday party. She didn't want to miss it. Lola looked exactly like her, from her mannerisms to her cute little dimple, and I know my mom looked at her with curiosity at how this adorable little imp's life was going to unfold.

Since the seizure, she walked with a cane. Even then, she had trouble. For the party, she bought a new wig. I hadn't seen her wear one since I was a teenager. She put it on and came in my room so I could help her style it. As I combed her hair and started to talk, I saw tears rolling down her face. I'd rarely seen my mom upset about her cancer. She handled it with such grace and dignity. But I think she was crying because she knew this birthday party was the last event in the girls' lives that she'd see. I'm sure she was thinking about future birthdays, graduations, first dates, weddings—just life—everything she'd miss as she passed into the unknown.

I gave her a hug and assured her that she looked beautiful. She had a wonderful time at the party.

Every weekend my mom was up to it, I took the girls to see her. The reality of her condition was sadly inescapable: she wasn't getting better. She quickly went from a cane to a walker. My dad had to get a video baby monitor to keep an eye on her when she napped. We feared she'd have another seizure. I helped my dad so he could run errands, go to the grocery store, and have a little time for himself.

Unless you've gone through something like this, you don't realize the way a serious illness gradually extends its tentacles into every aspect of daily life. As the cancer consumed my mom, it also took over our lives, too, especially my dad's. She couldn't be left alone. She struggled to walk. She passed out a few times. Her thinking was cloudy. Unable to lift a pan, she had to stop cooking, something that was like breathing to her. She was a nur- turer, yet now she was the one who needed full-time nurturing. Maybe this was the last lesson she needed to learn.

Nevertheless, we didn't give up hope. Even knowing the prognosis, I still hoped for a miracle. I think that's human nature.

A couple of my girlfriends insisted I needed a distraction,

a girls' night out. They were probably right; I'd turned into a homebody. They wanted to see the *American Idol* finale if possible, so I called Ryan Seacrest, who kindly arranged for amazing seats for us at the Kodak Theatre. On the way to the theater, though, I was hit by a wave of nausea. I didn't know what the hell was wrong with me. As I went through security at the theater, my fear of throwing up became an embarrassing reality. My hand went over my mouth and I turned bug-eyed. A guard asked if I was okay. I shook my head no, ran past him, and found a trash can in the corner of the lobby and threw up!

I hadn't thrown up since I was fifteen, and here I was, moments before a live broadcast of television's highest-rated show, on my hands and knees, puking on the floor. I was mortified. A nurse from first aid helped me into her office, where I vomited again.

I couldn't figure out why I was sick. I didn't feel as if I had the flu or even food poisoning. My friends insisted it was stress. "I have never thrown up from stress," I said. My friend said, "You have never had to deal with your mom dying of cancer." She was right. After keeping everything from Charlie to Richie to my custody fight and my mom's cancer locked up inside me, I reached my limit. It exploded out of me.

After a few minutes in the nurse's office—it was just like being back in school—I felt better enough to watch the show. I didn't want to ruin our night out. On our way to our seats, I said hello to the *Idol* judges, Simon Cowell, Paula Abdul, and Randy Jackson. I also waved to Ryan. However, soon after the show started, I began to feel anxious again. The queasiness returned to my stomach. Then I panicked. What if I threw up on live TV?

Since they often panned to celebrities in the audience, I knew there was a chance, however remote, of something dreadful being witnessed by thirty million people, and that slim possibility was enough for me to bid a hasty good-bye to my girlfriends and go home.

A few days later, Ryan interviewed me on his radio show. He asked what had happened to me at *Idol*. One minute he saw me in my seat, then I disappeared. I lied and said I hurried home after getting a call that one of my kids was sick. I thought that would be easier than explaining I'd puked in the lobby and thought it might be better if I didn't risk doing it again on the country's top-rated show.

Off the air, Ryan asked if I'd come into his office and meet with him and his producing partner about starring on a reality TV show. I agreed to meet, but I said, "No way will I do a reality show." I had more than enough reality in my life already, thanks very much.

5

ONE WEEKEND MY oldest nephew, Al, then twelve, came up for a couple of days of shopping, beach, and fun. We'd always been close and I was looking forward to hanging out together. As we were about to leave for lunch, my dad called, frantic. An ambulance was at the house. My mom had collapsed and was being taken to the hospital. She was in her second round of a new chemo that she hoped would be her miracle. It wasn't.

Within minutes, I had a bag packed, put all the kids in the car, and pulled onto the freeway. When I saw my mom in the emergency room, she was weak and her eyes were glazed and seemingly unfocused, though I had a feeling inside she knew what was going on. I'll never forget the look on her face; I wish it weren't etched in my memory. After a few minutes, her doctor took me aside and said he was going to stop her chemo, get her hydrated, and then let us take her home.

I turned toward her and then told him that she wasn't going home. "I don't think she'll make it out of the hospital," I said. He reassured me that she would.

I stood by myself, feeling a tremor of reality travel through my body. I knew the time had come to face the grim fact. It had been seven months since the doctor gave me her prognosis. My mom was dying. I saw a look in her eyes that hadn't been there before. I can't explain it further. Something was missing.

All the kids went back to my parents' house and I stayed at the hospital with my dad. My mom battled for three weeks. We were there every day. Her sister came out from Wisconsin and stayed with us, as did her best friend, Diane. One day my ex-boyfriend Pat came to see her. Sadly, Charlie didn't come say good-bye to my mom. We celebrated Thanksgiving, my mom's favorite holiday, in her hospital room. My sister also gave birth to her third son, John, and brought him to the hospital. My mom was barely coherent, yet I know she saw him. That meant a lot to my sister.

Two days before my mom passed away, she was alert, which the nurses told us was common. Maybe it's God's way of allowing time to say good-bye. My mom was such a proud, brave woman, and I know she didn't like us seeing her sick and vulnerable. She was in and out of consciousness and on a morphine drip. I was terrified she would pass away when I was at the house with my girls. She was my biggest fan, my number one supporter, my confidante, and my rock. I wanted to be there with her at the end, providing all of the same.

The next day I held her hand for hours as she drifted in and out of consciousness. At one point, when I knew she was awake and listening to me tell her how much I loved and appreciated her, I simply said, "Please don't wait for me to leave the room and then go." I never wanted to use the word "death." I didn't want to say "when you die." She remained silent, but I knew she heard. "Mom, you were there when I entered the world, and I want to be with you when you go."

Knowing we were near the end, we all slept at the hospital in her room that night. At 4:30 a.m. on November 30, my sister left to be with her family. We all looked at my mom. Even though she was still breathing, the nurse could not get a pulse. She tried again with the same result. "The oxygen mask is helping her breathe, but she is almost on the other side," the nurse explained. My dad walked over to my mom, lifted her mask off, and kissed her forehead. I held my mom's hand and five minutes later she passed away.

I drove back to my parents' house, though I don't remember how I got from one place to the other. I was in disbelief. Every morning throughout my adult life I'd called my mom and we talked while having coffee. Who was I going to call at 7:00 a.m.? And my girls were never going to know her. That was a travesty. Early the next morning I walked into my parents' room and found my dad on the bed, sobbing as he looked through pictures of her. "She was too good of a person to go," he said. "It should've been me."

That destroyed me. I wrapped my arms around him, closed my eyes, and hung on, hoping both of us would find strength. When I gave birth to my daughters, I experienced a love that was deeper than any I could imagine. Death was similar—but the opposite. It was a feeling of loss I never knew existed—a deep, painful emptiness that I had to find my way through. And I knew I would, eventually. But at that moment, I was lost.

I drove back to my house to get something appropriate to wear for my mom's memorial and brought my aunt so I wouldn't have to sleep in my house by myself. The girls stayed with my dad overnight so he wouldn't have to sleep alone, either. In the middle of the night I woke up having what I thought was a heart attack. I couldn't breathe. I was hit by the full force of my mom being gone and the fact that I'd never see her again, never feel her hug or hear her voice comforting me with advice or an invitation to come home and let her fix me something to eat.

I spent the whole next day hunched over in pain, trying to catch my breath. At my mom's memorial, we displayed beautiful pictures of her everywhere and magnificent flower arrangements. My dad and I spoke. We barely made it through, but the dear friends and family members understood. I felt a part of me had died, too. From the day I was born my mom was always there, before friends, boyfriends, marriage. I didn't know life without my mom, and I certainly didn't want to imagine it without her. Yet now I had to figure out this next part of my journey on my own. I rued the tragic irony. When I needed her more than ever, she wasn't there.

Or so I thought. On the morning she died, I told her friend Diane that I didn't know how to tell the girls that their nana was in heaven. Diane produced a book. "I think this will help," she said, wiping a tear. Three months earlier, it turned out, my mom had bought two copies of *The Fall of Freddie the Leaf*, a book by Leo Buscaglia that teaches simply and clearly through a tree and the changing seasons that death is part of life. One copy was for my children and one was for Michelle's boys. My mom had sent them to Diane and told her to give them to my sister and me after she died. My dad didn't even know she had done this.

Well, inside the book my mom had written a personal note to Sam and Lola saying she had arrived in heaven and was fine, and she would always protect them. I almost fell over when I read it. I could not believe she was still helping me—still helping us. I needed the book at that time more than my kids. I marveled at my mom. After I quit crying, I looked up at the sky and said, "Thanks, Mom. I love you."

PART NINE

It's Not That Complicated

1

....

IN FEBRUARY 2008, almost three months after my mom passed away, E! announced *The Untitled Denise Richards Show* was set to start production and air that summer. The premise was simple. Cameras would follow me in and out of my home as I raised my children and pursued my career as an actress while also recovering from a messy Hollywood divorce and the loss of my mother. The series fit in perfectly on a network schedule whose hits were *The Girls Next Door* and *Keeping Up with the Kardashians*. In other words, women tuned in. As Lisa Berger, E!'s executive vice president, said, "At the core of this series is a resilient single mom who is trying to get her life back on track."

Resilient?

I hoped so.

Trying to get my life back on track?

That was the point—and no matter how much of the show would end up being "produced," the reality of my reality was a part of every decision long before contracts were even signed. As I said earlier, I told Ryan Seacrest that I wasn't interested in doing a reality series. I was an actress, with a résumé of movie and TV credits; I was having a hard enough time getting a job and thought a reality show might make it worse. But once Ryan called and talked it through with me, I had a different opinion and recognized that it could actually be a good thing. Also, I felt that more than enough of my real life was being captured in the media. I couldn't go outside without paparazzi pointing still and video cameras at me. There were photos of me at the grocery store, driving car pools, filling up at the gas station, entering or exiting the courthouse, taking the girls out to dinner, even going to the doctor. How much more could I expose?

As I told Ryan, I was trying to protect my privacy. I'd been ripped to pieces in the press. I felt as if everyone hated me. I was embroiled in an ongoing custody battle. My mom was in the final stages of a losing fight against cancer. And on top of everything else, I didn't feel good—or rather, didn't like where I was in my life at that moment. I'd gained weight, I wasn't social, and I'd pretty much lost all my confidence. My self-esteem was shot. With all I'd been through, I felt beaten and bruised. I was the last person on the planet who needed to put her private life on TV.

On camera, Ryan exudes a boyish, best-friend type of charm, and he's no less friendly in person. But off camera, in his office, he's a savvy businessman and a hands-on producer, which pleasantly surprised me. He listened to everything I said; I was excited at the prospect. But I still wanted to mull it over.

Aside from mulling it over with my agent, I went to my mom. My mom thought Ryan was adorable, the all-American boy-next-door type that neither of her daughters brought home, and when I told her that he wanted to produce a reality show starring me, she saw it as an opportunity. I remember being in her kitchen over coffee. "Really?" I asked. She nodded and said, "It might be good for you." When I ran through all the shit that was

going on in my life, all the reasons not to do the show, she shook
her head. "You're stronger than you think," she said. "People
need to get to know the real you."

By the time negotiations started, my mom had taken a turn
for the worse. I negotiated most of the deal while sitting on my
mom's bed in her hospital room. At the time, we were still hoping and praying for a miracle, and so my vision, and the original
intention of the show, was to include my mom and dad. They
both wanted to be a part of it. I wanted to shoot at their house
as well as mine. I envisioned a reality show that was going to be
real. I'd been a fan of *The Osbournes*, particularly the ground-
breaking first season, whose addictive charm, I thought, was due
largely to their honest take on themselves as a family. I wanted
my series to be like that. Maybe not revolutionary; there wasn't
much new ground left to break in reality. But I wanted it to be
honest—and raw, if necessary. In addition to seeing me deal with
my career and children, I wanted people to see my mom's heroic
fight against cancer. I felt that it was something people could
relate to, and I expected her to beat it.

Unfortunately, she then took a dramatic, final turn for the
worse, was hospitalized, and never left. However, encouraged
by her to continue with the project, I finished negotiating the
deal from her hospital room. I had her support and approval.
She wanted me to do it. Even as she was dying, she fueled me
with strength. "Keep picking yourself up," she said. She knew
my reality. In addition to everything else going on, my attorney
fees were draining my bank account and I needed a paycheck.
"I'm not worried about you," my mom said. "You'll be fine." I
heard that over and over as she held my hand. Instead, she was

concerned about my father and her dog, Sheena. "Promise me that you'll take care of them," she said. I squeezed her hand. "I will," I said.

After she died, I could easily have backed out of the show. I had an understandable excuse. But despite my sadness, my mom, in some strange kind of way I didn't fully understand yet, had left me feeling strong and good about the show even though I didn't feel strong and good about much else. Later, following the memorial, in those difficult days when my dad and I sat around and cried and I found myself calling her cell phone just to hear her voice, I had a moment where time seemed to stop. I saw clearly where I was at that point. My life stood out like a 3-D landscape: problems here, challenges there, responsibilities all around, risks ahead of me, and maybe opportunities, too. I didn't know. But I made a stark and frank assessment, and I did something that was very much me, but also very much something my parents had taught me my whole life, and that was to face the facts and fix the things I didn't like. I had to remake my life.

When I was growing up, and especially during my teenage years, my dad repeatedly told my sister and me that life was what you made of it, and so many times in the past when the cards didn't go my way, or I felt that they didn't, I realized he was right. And now those words rang truer than ever before. I heard them loud and clear, as if I were a kid instead of a grown woman, and once again I realized he was right.

It was up to me to make changes. It was simple advice, but true. If I didn't like my life, I had to face the facts and then do something about it. Another realization I want to pass on: I didn't look back at events that were within my control with regret. I just had more work to do. Lots more. In fact, I had a whole list: I had to climb out of my depression. I needed to make money. I wanted the negative press to start changing and for people to discover the real me. I also wanted to get my ass in gear, physically, emotionally, and socially. It would only help my girls if I was happier and healthier.

And workwise, well, my career was in the toilet. It was hard for me to accept that my personal life had affected my livelihood. But few people casting new movies and TV shows had me at the top of their list. So for reasons that can best be described as "all of the above," I decided to move ahead with the reality show. I knew it could go either way. But I had nothing to lose. Things could only get better.

2

THAT DIDN'T MEAN they'd get easier.

I don't like when people giving advice make it seem as if all you have to do is think positive, snap your fingers, and life changes. It doesn't. God knows, I don't have special powers. Real change is a process of taking baby steps and going over speed bumps. Shortly before production began, I got into a minor dustup with Charlie about whether the kids could be in the show. He'd agreed, then changed his mind, and blah-blah-blah. Although we quickly resolved the disagreement, the press worked it up into a piece that made it appear I was an awful mom exploiting the girls for my own benefit. I felt that I couldn't catch a break.

It only emboldened my resolve to show people a sense of who I really was. In short order my house was transformed into a set. Lights were installed, producers mapped out each room, there were meetings and discussions about my life, and then the crew arrived. On nearly every one of my previous jobs I'd felt an affinity for the crew. They arrived earlier and stayed later than everybody else, and typically they were a bunch of fun people. My kids especially loved when my gym was turned into the production office. Craft service was there, and they loved the people with all the snacks. The first couple days of shooting, when we wrapped, my girls would go into the production room and sneak out saying, "Mom, the people left all their candy." They said it as if the people had left all their expensive jewels. It was funny. On the first day of production of my show, I introduced myself to everyone and set out food in the kitchen. I wanted them to feel comfortable. But they were standoffish, and I didn't get it. As we got under way, I kept cracking jokes and talking to them without getting any reaction. Between one quick setup, I turned toward one guy and said, "I heard you have kids." He nodded. "Boys or girls?" I asked. No response. I thought, "Whoa, this is going to be a long season. It's going to suck."

Finally, the director stopped filming and took me into another room. "You can't talk to the crew," she said.

I took a step back. "What do you mean I can't talk to them?"

"On reality shows, they don't interact with the talent. They're supposed to be background, almost invisible."

I shook my head, not angry but firm. "Then you're working with the wrong person. These people are in my home. This is very personal. I'm going to talk to them. I can't feel like I'm being an asshole by ignoring them." She tried to offer a rebuttal, but I interrupted, "I'm sorry. I can't not talk to them." By the end of the season, they were eating my dad's chicken nuggets and we would have dinner with them.

Coming from movies and scripted TV, I was used to scene-by-scene direction and hitting certain marks, but on the reality show I was told to go wherever I wanted and do whatever I planned on doing, which struck me as bizarre. It took a while to adjust. In a way, though, that was a perfect metaphor for what I was trying to do with my life. I had to toss out the old way of doing things, forget about the places I used to stand, and create a new vision for myself.

That new vision included a familiar last name. The opening episode showed me changing my last name back to Richards, but it didn't fully capture my frustration when that seemingly simple task turned into a bureaucratic nightmare. I'd had to wait four years or until my divorce from Charlie was granted in the court system, which meant I was Denise Sheen longer than I was actually married. So with cameras following me, I went to the DMV to change my driver's license and all the corresponding paperwork. After I waited in line, the woman behind the counter looked over my paperwork and shook her head no. I needed my court-approved divorce decree, she explained. "It's our policy," she added.

I couldn't believe it. "Come on," I said. "My divorce has been everywhere, on the news. You know I'm divorced."

She nodded. "From Charlie Sheen."

"See. You know."

"But I need to see the official court papers. That's our policy."

A few days later, I returned with the legal document, waited in the same line, and saw the same lady. To my disbelief, I received another shake of her head. This time, after scrutinizing my divorce papers, the woman pointed out that the judge had failed to stamp my divorce decree.

"So even though it says I'm divorced, even though the judge signed it, you can't process my name change?" I asked.

"Nope. Not unless it's stamped." I stared at her, frozen. Begging her. She was not swayed. "It has to be stamped."

Now, Charlie was about to marry his girlfriend, Brooke Mueller. Their engagement and upcoming nuptials were all over the news. "This isn't fair," I said. "My ex-husband is allowed to get remarried but I'm not able to change my last name? I still have to be Denise Sheen?" She nodded yes. Whatever . . . still doesn't make sense to me, but I was at the mercy of the DMV.

After my attorneys took the papers back to the judge, I made another trip to the DMV. The third time was the charm. At home, my dad congratulated me. He whipped up a celebratory dinner, one of his three-course specialties.

That was another problem. After being married to my mom for thirty-seven years, he was lost without her. They'd sold their coffee shop when she got sick; his life was about taking care of her, as he squeezed every possible minute of companionship before she was gone. Then his life fell apart and I had to be there for him. At my insistence, he moved into my house right before production started. The timing was perfect. Being around the girls helped him through the worst of the pain, and he enjoyed hanging out with the show's crew. In a way, it was a godsend to have so many people in the house every day.

He took over the cooking chores with the gusto of a man with a renewed purpose. At breakfast, he planned lunch and dinner. While he was skilled in the kitchen, he only knew how to cook multicourse feasts. Every meal was Thanksgiving dinner—meat and potatoes and dessert. My dad was a rail. He'd never worried about weight in his life. However, I ended up gaining about ten to fifteen pounds. It was the first time in my life I added padding where I didn't want any. I began to look at the bowl of mashed potatoes as my enemy. I forced myself to decline seconds when, in truth, nothing made me feel better than a heaping spoonful of spuds whipped with butter and showered in salt. I knew I was going to have to start hitting the gym. Ugh.

My body needed more work than that. I also visited tattoo artist Kat Von D., who transformed the tattoo of Charlie's name on my ankle into a beautiful, and feminine, fairy. It hurt like hell. But I expected as much. Changing your life, like a tattoo, isn't easy—or without pain.

3

....

AS WE FINISHED episodes and the airdate neared, I fretted about the obvious risk of doing a reality show at this tenuous point in my life. What if nobody watched? What if people didn't like me? What if being myself wasn't good enough? What if it didn't go over? Would low ratings mean I would never, ever work again? Was I doing the right thing? Was I setting myself up for failure?

These were all normal concerns people have when they venture to remake their lives. Hey, talk to any woman who starts to emerge from her shell after a divorce. It's not easy showing up at your kid's classroom as a single parent or going to a party with friends as a third wheel. Doing all that on TV just magnified the risks, though I only had myself to blame if it failed.

Fortunately, it didn't. Though I was grilled about everything but my new TV series when I promoted it on shows such as *Today* and CNN's *Larry King Live*, more than 1.5 million people tuned into *It's Complicated* when it debuted in May 2008. E! considered it a success. Mail and e-mail poured in. As I'd hoped, the show struck a nerve among a group of viewers who settled in front of their TV sets on Sunday nights. Judging from the comments I received, many saw someone like themselves in me or someone they knew. They identified with me. "Denise, I do the same thing," one note said. Others shared stories of their divorces. "Hang in there, girlfriend," another wrote.

Relieved to have support instead of criticism, my spirits and self-confidence slowly started to build. People related to me and my family, especially my dad. Despite some of the corny scenes that were set up, they got to know me. They saw me with my friends, my dad, and my children, and they liked what they saw, which was exactly what I needed after two years of thinking the world hated me.

The fifth episode, titled "Saying Good-bye," dealt with my mom's death, and not surprisingly it garnered the biggest reaction. It was also the most authentic of all the episodes, too. It came about after the director observed my dad and me off camera still grieving my mom and suggested we deal with it on camera. I debated whether I wanted to show that much of my life. It seemed too personal. There had to be limits. But then I thought, why not? We were going through this painful process—maybe other people going through the same thing would be comforted seeing they weren't the only ones crying or calling a loved one's cell phone just to hear his or her voice again.

After my dad and sister agreed to share these intensely personal emotions, which took a lot of guts, cameras followed us down to Encinitas and into my parents' house. It was the first time Michelle and I had gone there since my mom passed. All three of us had a difficult time going inside. We felt my mom's absence in every room. My sister and I went through my mom's closet and drawers looking for favorite items to turn her clothes into memory bears for our children.

My dad and I gave Sami and Lola their special bears one afternoon as they were having a tea party. They were made from an old pair of denim pants and shirt. I told the girls they were special gifts that "would always remind them of Nana." They reached out, their faces lighting up as if my mom were giving them the gifts herself. "How pretty!" Lola said. "I love it," Sami added.

I tried my best not to break down. "Whenever you want, you can talk to Nana," I said. "She'll always be with you."

Lola looked up at me with her wide eyes that reminded me of my mom. "My angel?"

"Yes, your angel," I said.

Afterward, I was pleased with myself for doing that episode. Again, it opened a door few people knew how to go through. Death is a subject rarely spoken about, and grief is similarly neglected. Not for lack of interest. I think it's more about fear—

fear of the unknown, fear of the pain and what the deep sorrow of loss and grief feels like. After my mom, a few people did speak to me about their experiences and asked me about the feelings I was experiencing, and it was helpful. Talking and sharing was cathartic, and they jump-started the hard process of healing. Likewise, in the same way I'd found it helpful when I was pregnant to talk to girlfriends who'd had a baby, I talked to friends who'd lost a parent. I found it therapeutic to open up with girlfriends who'd gone through breakups and divorces, who were single moms raising children on their own, and who'd worked up the nerve to get their asses back into the world.

Talk is good, especially when it's real and substantive and addressing subjects that might turn into debilitating fears and secrets if kept bottled up. It's equally good to chat about the tiny, everyday stuff, such as the brand of shampoo or beauty products you have on the bathroom counter, a fabulous farmers' market in the neighborhood, or a good summer camp for the kids. In those discussions I'm always reminded of how similarly most of us live. Anyway, I'm a talker, and I hadn't done much of that since my life had turned into a nonstop soap opera after I got together with Richie. Even though it took doing a reality show to open me up, the resulting conversations had a positive effect.

We did an episode in Hawaii where I refused to get into a bikini and took heat in the tabloid press for looking chunkier on the sand, but as soon as the season ended, I put myself on a disciplined exercise regimen, starting at 5:00 a.m. when I gulped a cup of coffee and my Pilates instructor had me on my reformer getting my ass in shape.

Besides getting into better shape, I made other changes. I moved to a four-bedroom, two-story Cape Cod–style home in Pacific Palisades. I wanted to be closer to town and thought the girls might like living by the beach. I also used that time to figure out where I really wanted to settle before they started kindergarten. But when I look back at what was behind my decision that summer, I can see another reason I moved, a reason not readily apparent to me but one stemming from the risks I'd taken and the work I was doing on myself. I wanted light in my life.

I know that might sound a little too New Agey for some, as it would for me, but that's not the way I mean it. I literally wanted light. I was ready to step out from the darkness of the past few years. I thought it would be nicer living closer to the ocean. I didn't realize fog fills the sky much of the year, but, hey, that was a technicality; and as things turned out, I moved back to my old neighborhood a year later. But the change was a fun distraction that got me thinking about how I wanted my life to look. I don't think there's anything wrong with devoting time and energy to your surroundings. I encourage it. I am constantly working on a project, redecorating a room, renovating a house, rearranging my closet, doing something that makes me feel good. It can be as little as lighting a wonderfully aromatic candle, or taking forty-five minutes out to get a manicure, or meeting a friend for a long, leisurely lunch, or sitting on the beach with the kids in the last warm rays of the day's sunshine, or curling up with a good book.

An insight that took me time to rediscover: life's short, and we're all adults. If you get the urge to redecorate a room, your house, or your entire life, do it.

4

....

IN JANUARY 2009, I flew to Utah for the Sundance Film Festival to help promote a small, offbeat romantic comedy I was in called *Finding Bliss.* As I got off the plane, my *It's Complicated* crew met me. It was the first time I'd seen them since the previous summer. Now we were starting the second season. I gave one guy a big hug and turned to the camera and explained, "This is my crew!" I saw the director. "Everyone knows there are cameras following me," I said. On the second season we actually broke the third wall and talked into the camera a lot of the time. Since I did it a lot with the crew, when the producers saw dailies, they actually liked it. Probably annoyed I was still Chatty Cathy with our crew, but whatever. I still did it.

If keeping it real was my new mantra, I was happy to see return another part of my life—my sense of humor. Before the *Finding Bliss* press conference, I was chatting with my costar Jamie Kennedy. He asked if I had any idea what questions reporters might ask us about the movie. "I wish they'd ask me about the movie," I said. "They'll just ask about my social life and my relationship with Charlie." As for Jamie, I thought it was pretty obvious what the press would ask him, too. Then I realized something. "You haven't seen the movie yet, have you?" I asked.

He shook his head. "Why?"

I smiled.

"Does my pickle show?" he asked.

I nodded. Jamie played a young porn star in this movie about an enterprising young filmmaker who enters the business through the adult-film industry. One scene included a full-frontal peek at his pickle. "Oh my God," he said facetiously. I laughed. Having done nudity on-screen, I assured him there was nothing to worry about, as long as he kept his parents from seeing the movie—and from looking at websites that would post screen grabs.

A little more than a month into shooting the second season of *It's Complicated*, I took another risk. I joined ABC's hit series *Dancing with the Stars*. Yes, gulp. It seemed from the time the show debuted in 2005 they had invited me to participate, and each time I politely declined. The reason? I wasn't a dancer. Oscar-winning choreographer Debbie Allen had her hands full when she prepared Charlie and me for our first dance, and prior to that my only real experience with anything resembling dance moves was pom-pom girls and cheerleading, and if you recall, my career came to a teary end in eleventh grade when I didn't make the team. But I said yes this time for a couple reasons.

First, Sami and Lola, who were fans of the show and enjoyed dressing up in costumes with sparkles and fixing their hair, like me, had started taking gymnastics lessons. They seemed like naturals to me, but they were shy about doing routines the first few times. They expected to be perfect out of the gate. I tried explaining that nobody starts out perfect and that having butterflies is normal, but they had a hard timing understanding. Then the *Dancing* offer arrived and I thought, perfect, I'll show them Mommy goes through the same thing.

Selfishly, I'd noticed many of the *Dancing* participants got in great shape from doing the show. That sounded good to me. I also simply thought it would be fun to learn how to dance. Looking back, it would've been more fun to take private lessons instead of doing it in front of twenty-two million people. Oh, well, c'est la vie.

Like every other fan of the show, I waited eagerly for the rest of the cast to be announced. Except for a couple of the performers, I learned the names like everyone else did—well, most of them anyway. At the time, I was with a girlfriend in New York. I quickly read the names: Apple cofounder Steve Wozniak; rodeo champ Ty Murray; his wife, Jewel; Steve-O; football star Lawrence Taylor; singer Belinda Carlisle; country singer Chuck Wicks; Nancy O'Dell; rapper Lil' Kim; David Alan Grier; actor Gilles Marini; and—

"Here's the winner," I said.

"Who?" my girlfriend asked.

"Shawn Johnson. She's the Olympic gymnast. She won a gold medal and a silver."

"And you think she's going to win?"

"Yup."

I was partnered with Maksim Chmerkovskiy, the handsome, fiercely competitive dance champion. We met for the first time on *Good Morning America*—not even in the greenroom, but on the air—where we promoted the new lineup of stars. We hit it off right away. I thought he was sexy, obviously an amazing dancer, and funny. We had the same sense of humor.

On and off camera, I mentioned I was nervous but hoped to have fun anyway. Maks told me not to worry. But he told me he'd be mad if I got nervous . . . um, okay. Welcome to Maks's sense of humor.

The mistake I made in agreeing to go on *Dancing* was doing it at the same time I was shooting my reality series. It was too much and made every day a scheduling nightmare. Starting from the moment I left *Good Morning America*, *Dancing* required an intense time commitment and concentration, and to do well with my nonexistent dance background I needed to devote more time and energy than I had.

The first two weeks of rehearsals were great—then not so great. Maks and I were best pals during our three-hour lunch breaks, but our friendship was strained on the dance floor. The problem? Our approaches were different. Ask anyone and they'll tell you I'm disciplined and a hard worker, and I wanted to learn how to dance. But without any experience, I wanted to start with simple steps, not complicated routines. Maks disagreed. He had his way of teaching and long story short, after one particularly physically and emotionally grueling rehearsal, I asked my construction worker brother-in-law if he would bring over a sledgehammer and break my ankle. "It'll hurt less," I said.

5

....

THANK GOODNESS MAKS and I liked each other outside the studio. The camaraderie with all the participants was the best part. I loved the entire cast. As we rolled up to the season premiere, Shawn Johnson still looked to me like the front-runner. Gilles Marini, who became a good friend, also looked super, and I suspected he had some dance experience. If not, he was a natural. I picked him to give Shawn a run for the title. As for the pros, Derek Hough was amazing to watch and awesome at finding the strengths in every partner. You could tell he had a talent for making each dance about them, not himself. Cheryl Burke was similar—amazingly skilled at bringing out the best in her partner. Kym Johnson is one of the nicest women I've met and has the hottest body!

However, all of the pros impressed me. They were genuinely nice people, patient, immensely fun to watch close-up, and thrilled at the opportunity to have their talents put in the spotlight.

With a week to go before the season opener, the atmosphere behind the scenes turned intense. The effort took a toll. Jewel withdrew with what she thought was tendonitis. It turned out she had fractured tibias in both legs. Then Nancy O'Dell dropped out with a torn meniscus, which required knee surgery. Former *Bachelor* contestant Melissa Rycroft and *Girls Next Door* Playmate Holly Madison stepped in as last-minute replacements.

Ignoring reports of the *Dancing* curse, Maks pushed me to my limit and beyond as we worked on our first dance, the cha-cha. One day I simply cracked. I backed up against the mirror and slid to the floor, crying. Word got out, and Maks was accused of driving yet another partner to tears. I didn't blame him. I put pressure on myself. I wanted to do well. I also didn't want to embarrass myself on live TV.

On the flip side, I was in heaven with all the sequins, heels, eyelashes, spray tans, and costumes. It was the best kind of dress-up game, and I shared it all with Sam and Lola. On Sunday, we did an extensive run-through for the director and cameras. It was a full day of blocking. Early the next morning, everyone was ferried to the studio, where we rehearsed with the live band for the first time, spent the rest of the day getting dolled up and dressed, and then, finally, it was showtime.

I'll let you in on a not-so-little secret: never mind the twenty-million-plus people watching at home, I freaked out at the idea of dancing in front of the studio audience. Though a novice dancer, I was going to attempt to pull off a complex routine that would've tested someone who'd cha-cha-ed for years, and when our turn arrived, my nerves were as apparent as my spray-on tan. I didn't feel confident in my dance, and consequently I never relaxed. "You looked terrified out there," said judge Carrie Ann Inaba, and Bruno Tonioli agreed. "You've got it all, but you don't know what to do with it," he said. They were spot-on, of course. But I'd just wanted to make it through the routine. No flubs, no falls, no problem.

During week two, Maks was nicer. "Look at you, you're becoming a little ballroom dancer," he said in one rehearsal. "I'm so proud of you." On the show, the judges noted an improvement, too. "Much better," said Carrie Ann. "You were together," added the third judge, Len Goodman. "Well done." Though pleased, I had trouble the following week with the samba, which Bruno compared to a waffle, and I was sent home. Talk about relief. It was the first time I breathed easily in nine weeks.

The next morning I broke the news to Sam and Lola. They were delighted I no longer had to spend my days rehearsing.

Sam just had one question: "Does this mean you don't get the trophy?" No, I didn't, I explained. But there were other rewards. First and foremost, I'd provided my daughters a lesson in facing your fears, and I'd showed myself that I had the courage to step outside my comfort zone. It was okay to be afraid, but you couldn't let fear stop you.

In the process, I'd also lost an inch in my waist, dropping from a 26 to a size 25 jeans! My stomach was also flat and my legs and butt were rock hard. I wasn't eating any less, either. I was just in better shape.

Maks was the first person I called. I thanked him profusely for my new jeans size. He was also amused when I confessed that, despite our battles in rehearsals and my early elimination from the show, I'd fallen in love with dancing—and didn't plan to stop.

My friend Lisa Rinna had also turned into a dance fanatic after competing on the second season of *Dancing*, and she took me to a class taught by *DWTS* veteran Louis Van Amstel, who coached many of the show's pros. In the class, we did all the dances they did on the show, including the cha-cha, the samba, the quickstep, and the paso doble, except you didn't need a partner. It was a fantastic workout, with none of the pressure of the show. I didn't check my watch once the whole hour. After one session, I was hooked. I still go.

After *Dancing*, I wrapped season two of *It's Complicated*, and when I finally had a few moments to myself when I could stop and take stock of the whirlwind my life had been since my mom's turn for the worse, I was pleased about where I'd ended up. I was a little surprised, too. My mom had insisted I'd get through all the obstacles I faced, and when I didn't see how, she'd simply said I was stronger than I thought, I'd figure it out, and as I thought about it now, I guessed she was right.

I still wasn't at the top of anyone's list for movies or TV, but I accepted that my career as I neared forty might not be the same as it was at twenty-five. It could still be great, and with all that I'd been through, I felt that I could bring even more depth to a part. For the time being, though, my personal life was higher on my list of priorities, and I felt stronger and more confident than I had in years. I still had a ways to go. Who's ever done growing and evolving? I don't think I'll ever be finished. And with kids, I had more growing and evolving ahead of me than I could possibly imagine. I didn't even want to think about my little cuties hitting puberty, dating, and doing God only knows. For the time being, though, I was pointed in the right direction. My two gambles—doing a reality TV series and saying yes to *Dancing*—had paid off. The lesson? I'd taken control of my life instead of waiting for things to happen. My zest for life returned. I laughed more. I went out and socialized without worrying about the whole world hating me. People were starting to get to know the *real* me. I'd joined Twitter, which terrified me, opening myself up for people to tweet me whatever message they wanted to. I was so humbled and pleasantly surprised by the number of supportive messages and shocked that my followers are more than two million. They were a huge inspiration for writing this book.

PART TEN

·

Getting Work Done

1

....

IN EARLY JUNE 2009, as I left for New York to promote season two of *It's Complicated*, my publicist, Jill, booked me onto Howard Stern's radio show. She'd always turned down his invitations, but this time, she explained, she couldn't think of a reason to say no. "What more could someone ask you?" she said.

What more could he ask? There were the interviews most people did, and then there were Howard's interviews. That's what made him Howard. He asked questions no one else dared to ask. His Q&As skipped the boring stuff everyone else did and got right to the spicy questions where his subjects found themselves revealing the most surprising and intimate details; and if you weren't self-confident and willing to answer questions honestly, you'd best not show up to Howard Stern. So it was a measure of where I was in my life and the progress I'd made in rebuilding my self-confidence and sense of humor that I arrived in New York actually looking forward to sitting across from him.

Privately and publicly, I'd talked about the importance of owning your life, your entire life, the good and the mistakes, and learning from both, and as I knew, there was no better litmus test than a grilling from Howard Stern. I knew he'd ask about Charlie, but knowing Howard, I figured he'd skim over that well-worn subject and head straight to questions about the bedroom. No problem. I didn't know how much detail I'd offer or how much he'd ask for, but I had done my share of sexy magazine shoots and had no issues acknowledging that I enjoyed the sensual side of a relationship. Look, as a grown woman I made no bones that great sex is important. I wasn't afraid of anything he might ask, and that was a good, healthy feeling in itself.

That morning, I woke up early in my hotel room, put on a sexy red dress and high heels, looked at myself in the mirror, and thought I wouldn't have worn that outfit for the *Today* show, but I knew what Howard liked, as well as what his audience expected. In the car that took me to the studio, I was relaxed and looking forward to having fun, a nice change from previous press tours where I was on guard and defensive.

On most radio shows, you are ushered into the studio during a break and introduced to the host. At Howard's, it's different. I was taken into the studio while he was on the air, and he drew me right into the conversation. It was my first time meeting Howard, who described me to his listeners and then jumped right into the interview. I don't remember the order of questions, but he only touched on my ex briefly before getting to one of his favorite topics. "Are your breasts real?" he asked. "Are they natural?"

I laughed. "They're natural on the outside. I'm not going to lie to you because I'll never hear the end of it."

Howard cocked his head. "So you had the operation?"

I adjusted myself on his sofa. "A long time ago. I've had a few."

Within hours of my response, the Internet was full of stories about my boob job, as if an operation I'd had twenty years earlier was news. In a way, though, it was. Until Howard's show, I'd never spoken about my first boob job—or the second or third. Not because I tried to hide that I'd had surgery or because I was embarrassed. The truth was, no one had ever asked. (Obviously that's what makes Howard outstanding at his job.) But I have strong opinions about plastic surgery, as you might imagine—as it relates to your right to look the way that will give you the most self-confidence and also in terms of the precautions you need to take.

Can plastic surgery help you remake yourself as you desire? Sometimes. Striving to be your best self is part of your journey, and some days your boobs are as important as your brain. I know that sounds funny, but self-esteem is like the circuit box that connects all the different parts. Sometimes you want to feel smart. Other times you want to feel sexy. Does having implants or your nose fixed make you any less real? No, not at all. It can make you feel better—much better. Can you get a bad doctor? Can you cross the line where you have too much work done? Well, you know the answer to that as well as I do. We've heard the stories, and we've seen the casualties. How do you know when you're good, when to leave well enough alone? You just do, hopefully. My experiences encompass a bit of everything. Let me tell it to you.

My sister was blessed with a natural C-cup. I was not and, of course, grew up a wee bit envious. All through junior high and high school, I waited to develop, and didn't, and as a result, boys made fun of my chest. I had heard all their derogatory remarks—and they hurt. I was an A-cup. I wanted to be bigger—especially after I moved to L.A. I wish I had been more confident about my body back then.

My roommate at the time had a fabulous figure—and great boobs. One night we were talking and I mentioned being self-conscious about my flat chest. Stephanie, who had fabulous, round, perfect breasts, confessed to having had hers done before moving to L.A. I was surprised and then intrigued as she suggested that I get mine done, too, if I wanted to be bigger. I glanced down at myself. Call me naïve, but until that moment I'd never thought that I could go out and buy new breasts. I mean, I had heard of women getting them done, but I had just never known anyone. Then I couldn't get the idea out of my head.

Able to afford an operation with the money I'd scraped together from modeling, I decided that I'd fill my A-cup with implants. Small implants. I didn't want to be huge. Just big enough to fill a nice B-cup bra. I pictured myself showing off curves in a bikini and wearing a bustier. What would that be like? How fun would that be?

My parents were not happy when they heard I'd met with a plastic surgeon. Neither was my modeling agent, who sounded like my parents when he warned against changing my physique. Both had their biases. Yet seeing I was determined to go ahead with it, my agent recommended a surgeon who had worked on other clients, though as I took the number down, he warned, "Don't get them too big."

I would advise anyone thinking of the same operation, especially at nineteen years old, the age I was at the time, to meet with several doctors and educate herself as thoroughly as possible before going ahead with the operation, as one should with any surgery. I didn't. Even though my parents were against it, they took me to the doctor's office on the morning of the surgery. I was terrified—not of the surgery but of throwing up as I came out of the anesthesia, which I'd heard was a common side effect. My doctor assured me that something would be put in my IV to prevent that from happening. Just before I was put under, I looked up at the doctor from the table and said, "Remember, I just want to be a little fuller. Not too big. A B-cup is fine."

When I woke up from surgery, I felt as if hot knives were stabbing my chest. I had the sensation of heaviness there, as if the doctor had stood on top of me while sewing me shut. I knew slicing my breasts open and stuffing them with silicone was going to cause a period of discomfort, but I wasn't prepared for the severity of the pain. They assured me that I had enough medication, which made me shudder at how bad it would've been without it, and I was surprised when I was sent home, bandaged and sore, later that afternoon.

My mom almost fell over when she saw me. The bandage around me was so thick she thought I was a double D. I wasn't *that* big, but I was close. When the swelling finally went down, I was close to a D. I was pissed. They were exactly what I didn't want. While I filled out a bikini and bustier like nobody's business, boobs that size were simply too big for my frame. I would've marched right back in and had them redone except for the pain of another operation.

2

....

INSTEAD I LIVED with them for several years. Then, while I was auditioning for *Wild Things*, which, if you recall, involved numerous callbacks, I learned the silicone in my breasts had hardened and my implants needed to be replaced. Perfect. Now I had to get them changed, and this time I'd make sure they were smaller. On the day before the operation, I was offered *Wild Things*. I didn't cancel. It was a huge risk since I was going topless in the movie. What if my boobs didn't look good?

I was dismayed when, a week after the surgery, the swelling went down and I found that my boobs weren't any smaller. In fact, they were even bigger. Despite my very specific instructions not to, the doctor had put in larger implants! The original pair were 255 cc; the latest pair were 275 cc! Upset that I'd gone through the operation for nothing, and in terrible pain, I flew to the movie's Florida location without being able to lift my arms over my head for two weeks. All I could do was pray the nude scenes would come at the end of the three-month shoot, giving me enough time to heal.

Years later, after I opened up about this experience on Howard Stern, a magazine writing about it brought in a so-called expert who called me a liar and said no doctor would put something in that I didn't want. Not true—and as far as I was concerned, that statement was irresponsible because it happened. The proof was on my chest. And you know what? There are a lot of botched plastic surgeries and surgeons doing what they think will look good, not what the patient wants.

I lived with my bigger boobies for a few years. It was difficult to wear clothes. My body was small, but with my big boobs I couldn't button tops. I had to buy bigger sizes and get them altered, which was a pain in the ass—and expensive. Also, from the chest up, I thought I looked heavy on camera. The problem was, my body was out of alignment and I didn't feel comfortable on camera or off.

Finally, after finishing press for the Bond film, I worked up the courage for surgery number three. This time I met with several surgeons, explained my prior experiences, which I compared to betrayals, and eventually found a doctor I trusted. I actually bought a B-cup bra and made the surgeon fit the implants in that damn bra.

Early that December, I went in for surgery. My boyfriend Pat and my parents took me to the appointment, then snuck me out the back door afterward since I was now more recognizable, and took me home, where I went through the same painful, hot-stabbing-knife recovery. After healing, I was finally happy with my size. I went from 275 cc to 180 cc. I could button my tops again!

After my mom passed away, my OB had me get a mammogram so we'd have a baseline in my records. He called it precautionary, since I was in excellent health, but one of the results came back sketchy and I needed another one, which made me nervous. After the second mammogram yielded equally uncertain results, I started freaking out, thinking I had breast cancer. By this time, I was battling a fear that I was going to die at a young age like my mom. I projected all sorts of terrible scenarios, all of which included missing my daughters' growing up.

Needless to say, I worked myself nervous. My sister drove to L.A. and accompanied me to my MRI, and then the two of us waited for the results at my house. I was a nutcase while waiting for the phone to ring. After a few hours, the doctor called: everything was fine—at least as far as my immediate worries. It turned out both of my implants were ruptured. There was no telling how that had happened, but I had to deal with it, which meant another surgery.

I consulted with an amazing female doctor who'd been described to me as an artist who happened to be a surgeon. I loved that she was a woman doing breasts, and from our first meeting I felt comfortable with her. In December 2009, I went in for my fourth surgery—my first since my daughters were born. At five and four, they were too young to understand but old enough to worry if they knew too much, so I told them I was having a minor procedure on my back. I know that sounds ridiculous to tell them I had back surgery, and they were quite curious as to why I had stitches in front, but somehow I convinced them. They had to go through the front to get to the back. Makes sense to me, right?!

My surgery took double the estimated time. My doctor said it was one of the worst ruptures she'd seen. Despite being under for hours, I woke up feeling great. I dubbed my anesthesiologist Dr. Feelgood. Wanting to avoid my girls those first few days when I was groggy, achy, swollen, and bandaged, I recovered at a private facility. It was like a Four Seasons hotel with nurses. Men and women walked around healing from various procedures, including nose jobs, face-lifts, lipo, and boob jobs. For most, their surgeries had been elective. I wondered whether they were finally addressing longtime issues or avoiding the inevitable. There's a difference. Obviously I'm not against plastic surgery. I'd be a hypocrite if I said anything against it. If you're considering a procedure, do as much research as possible, get several opinions, and don't rush. Take your time finding the right doctor. I only wanted my breasts done; it took four surgeries and nearly two decades before I was finally satisfied, and healthy.

Do some women go too far? It's not my place to judge, but when I see someone whose features have dramatically changed, I wonder if there aren't other issues that need to be addressed to find peace of mind. I'm hoping I won't want a lift or a snip when I'm seventy. I just hope I get there. If I reach that age, I'll be thrilled to be alive. I'm more concerned about watching my children grow up than I am about my face or anything else succumbing to gravity. Perspective—that's the key.

I stayed in that plush recovery spa for four days. At home, I wore a big shirt and a postsurgery bra. The girls thought my back was in a lot of pain. I spent a couple days in bed, propped up with pillows, catching up on my favorite TV shows. A week later, I was able to drive. By February, I was able to do light lower-body workouts. Now my breasts are the size and shape I wanted back when I was nineteen, though I wish I'd felt confident enough with my body to have never had surgery in the first place. It would've saved me a lot of pain and money.

For the record, I haven't had any other operations. Nor will I. I'm done. As I said, I don't care about defying age. My goal is to live a long and full life, and I'll take all the wrinkles God wants to give me if I can watch my children and their children grow up.

3

....

I NEVER HAD to worry about my weight until my dad moved in with me after my mom died and took over the cooking. Not one to deprive myself, I ate everything he served, relying on my metabolism to burn up the calories, just as it always had. But something happened. Either my body chemistry suddenly changed or I consumed more than my internal furnace could handle. One day I woke up fifteen to eighteen pounds heavier than I was when I bought everything in my closet. Nothing fit the way I wanted, in a way that felt comfortable, which was the way the rest of my life was going at the time. Without my mom, fighting with Charlie, and remaking my life, I wasn't comfortable.

It made me finally understand emotional weight. I have plenty of friends who look for comfort in what they consider the four basic food groups—sugar, salt, dairy, and starch. One bad phone call, argument, or disappointment and you can hear the bag of chips being opened. Later, they punish themselves even more for eating when they should've been doing something constructive to improve the situation. No one's ever found long-term solutions in a bag of Oreos. Indeed, I've never been one of those who glide into the pantry looking for succor. But I was definitely feeling dark and heavy, and the heaviness went straight to my midsection and my thighs. It was textbook psychology 101: my way of protecting myself from the sadness and pain of losing my mom. It was also some kind of silent communication between my dad and me. The turkey and gravy and mashed potatoes were conduits through which we shared our feelings. "Pass the potatoes" was really code for "I'm hanging in there. It's going to take time."

When we shot an episode of *It's Complicated* in Hawaii, I refused to wear a bikini. It was the first time in my life I felt uncomfortable wearing a bathing suit. I wore shorts and a bikini top instead and incorporated my weight gain into the story line. We were a reality show, after all. It got even more real when paparazzi photos of me on the beach surfaced under headlines that were more like body blows: "She's Not Pregnant! She's Fat!" It was kind of sad at a size 4 I was portrayed as being fat but this is the reality of my business. It hurt my feelings and as much as I wished those editors would cut me some slack, it was a wake-up call—not that I needed waking up.

I did a photo shoot where I couldn't fit into the clothes the stylist had pulled for me. I had trouble wiggling into a pair of pants even when I was wearing Spanx. I was disgusted. I didn't want to be that girl who people saw and thought, "Holy shit, she let herself go."

The trainers I'd worked out with over the years had always told me to go by the way my clothes fit, not by weight. Forget what the scale says; listen to your body. It was great advice. I knew my body was talking to me. My barometer was a favorite pair of jeans, and they were telling me I needed to get in better shape. Luckily, I listened. By the time I finished shooting the second season of my reality show, I was tired of feeling as if my ass were dragging five seconds behind the rest of me. Do you know the feeling? I was dragging, not my best, and I didn't like it. Maybe it was a sign I was starting to heal—or wanted to. I didn't spend too much time analyzing it. I just knew I was ready for a change.

I was feeling like a fat fuck and I said to myself, "Enough! You can't sit here and complain. Do something about it." So I did. I got a trainer and made a commitment to get back into shape. I checked my schedule, figured out when I had to get the girls up and ready for school, what else was on my agenda, and found the only time available for a consistent workout was at 5:00 a.m. When my trainer said he was willing to start pre-sunrise, I had no choice but to get started.

Though I barely had time for a cup of coffee, I worked out six days a week. It took a while before I felt good. The first few weeks were tough. I had to push myself to get back into the routine. Sometimes I had to do more than push myself. The verbal war that was waged in my head was not pleasant to listen to. As I've repeatedly said, change is gradual and hard—and that's especially true at five o'clock in the morning.

When I signed up for *Dancing*, Maks whipped my ass further into shape, and I noticed the sweat and punishment paying off. I'll tell you what also helped: I made a conscious decision to cook my own meals. I didn't fire my dad from kitchen duty as much as I relieved him of responsibility for me. I reintroduced veggies, fruits, and salads, in small to moderate portions, back to the dinner table. If I did sample some of my dad's potatoes, I took a spoonful, not a bowl. I didn't deprive myself—and still don't. If I'm in a restaurant and feel like chips and guacamole, I order it. I just don't eat a pound of it. I returned to the way I used to eat. I fueled my body instead of feeding my emotions. I don't know how my dad, in his late fifties, stayed skinny. But he did. Good genes, I suppose.

Weight is a tricky and sensitive subject, not unlike plastic surgery, except you do the work yourself. As I said, listen to your body, not the scale. You can apply that method to almost anything: in most situations, if you listen to your inner voice and to your heart, you'll make the right decision. I know it's a cliché, but so what, it's true. I've tried to pay attention to the messages my body sends me, and as a result I feel better now physically, mentally, and spiritually than I did in my twenties, which, given everything I've been through, is proof enough for me that the simplest approach works best.

Back when I couldn't afford to hire a private trainer, I wanted to get in good, organized workouts, and I found inexpensive classes in kickboxing, aerobics, and mat classes with no cardio. When I made my first movie, *Tammy and the T-Rex*, I met an actress with the most killer body. She walked around eating celery, but she looked damn good. I asked if she worked out. She said, "Pilates." I'd never heard the word. "What the hell is that?" I asked.

Now I own a Pilates reformer. I bought it after Lola was born and still use it regularly. My sister prefers the mat workout. Either way, Pilates lengthens and stretches your body and, in my case, works muscles I never knew I had. It was the only exercise that flattened my tummy after having two C-sections—though I'm not fanatical about needing perfect abs, or perfect anything. That whole idea of perfection—what does that mean? What is it other than a sure way to drive yourself to permanent needless frustration?

I am more comfortable in my skin today than I was in my twenties, and I do much less worrying than I did back then. I think that comes with experience, and being confident and secure that I have a grasp of what's important. I also know that every woman, no matter her size or shape, has good days and bad days. I've been around some of the most beautiful women in the world, actresses and models, and I've heard them say, "God, I feel so ugly today." It's nothing you can see. It has to do with how they feel on the inside. That's why I constantly remind myself that if I tend to the way I feel emotionally and spiritually, my body will follow. If people focused on that, no one would diet.

But let me make a few confessions to ensure you know that I'm living in the real world:

- I love ordering mac-n-cheese with french fries off the kids' menu at hotels.

- My favorite sweet indulgence is Häagen-Dazs mint-chip ice cream.

- My cocktail of choice is a Belvedere Lemon Drop.

- There ain't nothing like a bowl of chips and guacamole, and I have a good recipe.

- At the movies I put M&M's in my popcorn and eat them together.

- My favorite go-to snack is pretzels.

- I don't work out every day. A good week now is five days, a bad week is one day, and a very bad week is zero.

- My least favorite part of my body is my stomach.

- My favorite body part? My arms. A close second are my expensive breasts.

- I'm pretty good at doing my own makeup.

- I still can't style my hair well.

- My spray tan makes me feel thinner.

- My hair color is naturally dark, dark blond; if you need proof, look at my daughters.

Those tidbits are fun, but lest anyone get the wrong impression, I take care of myself to feel healthy and balanced, but I also do it to make sure my girls have a healthy and balanced role model. Having grown up with a mom who was an exceptional role model, I know the influence my behavior has on them, good and bad. They are still young, but girls and young women—make that women of every age—are bombarded with messages in the media about how we should look and feel, as if there were one particular, right way. There isn't. The best way to feel is confident—confident within yourself, and with yourself. Between what I do for a living and the chaos that's permeated my personal life, it's been a challenge.

For my being on set, photo shoots, and red carpet events, Sami and Lola see me getting my hair and makeup done, stylists dressing me, a manicurist painting my nails, and even someone coming to the house to spray-tan me, and I want them to have a healthy outlook on self-image and their bodies, and I try to instill that, but I feel like such a hypocrite when they see me work.

I constantly explain that it's my job. When Mommy does photo shoots or acts, she's playing a character. It isn't real life.

One day, Sami was on set with me and asked, "Mom, why don't you do your own makeup when you work?" Her question surprised me. It was one of those straightforward, honest questions, asked without guile, which would only come from a kid. I didn't know what the hell to say. I had to take a moment and think about it. "They're professionals," I said finally. "It's their job. Just like Mommy's doing a job." I had no idea whether that was right or wrong in terms of what she was really asking. Maybe it did address her question. She seemed satisfied. At least I'd told her the truth. Later, I wondered what my mom would've said if I'd asked her for advice. As a child, I'd loved watching her do her makeup and polish her nails. I'm sure that's the origin of my girly-girl passions. At the same time, through most of my childhood, she didn't have any hair. Looking back, I realized that gave me perspective; my mom was so real. The best I can do for my girls is to be the same. The reality in this world is that people do judge on appearances, but for all the clothes, makeup, and tan you can possibly put on, it doesn't change who you are on the inside, which is where you have to do the most work.

I can already hear myself talking to my girls when they're teenagers worrying about pimples, hair, fashion, and their figures. You can be anything you want in life, I'll say, but the thing you want to strive for most of all is to be someone you like.

That's true at any age.

4

....

RESILIENCY IS A key concept in our house. Since my girls are young, I don't lecture about overcoming setbacks, putting one foot in front of the other, and looking forward instead of getting bogged down in the past. Instead, I try to teach by example—the same way my parents showed me, starting when we moved to California. After I split with Richie, I turned down every invitation that came my way. I didn't even want to answer the phone in case it was a friend pleading with me to go to dinner if only to get my sorry ass out of the house. I made excuses. I was busy or had kids' stuff. I found a reason to say no.

Only gradually did my agent and a few persistent friends force me out of my hermit phase, and then it was as if a switch went off. Why was I holing up inside? Yes, I was hiding out from the paparazzi and the likelihood of finding myself at the center of another scandalous story. I was too humiliated to show my face. The hardest thing for anyone coming out of a broken relationship is to arrive at a dinner party alone—and in the early days, I thought everyone would be whispering, "Look, there's that girl who stole her friend's husband." It took everything in me to keep going to my mommy-and-me classes with the girls. I was embarrassed, wondering what the other moms thought of me. But the reality was, there was never a scandal in the first place, I didn't steal my friend's husband, and I enjoyed going out and doing things—I loved being social—and so I said, "What the hell have I got to lose?" and I started to attend events and parties and even went on the occasional secret date.

By 2010, though, I wasn't the problem any longer. It was my dad. After he moved in with me, he rented out his and my mom's house in Oceanside. As we shot the reality show, he settled into a nice routine of cooking and handling the household chores. I enjoyed having him there, as well as the convenience of another adult in the house. Plus the girls didn't have a father at the house every day, so it was a bonus to have a grandfather who was present and involved. All the activity kept him occupied and gave him a purpose every day. We helped each other through a hard time.

But we faced another hard time when I finally broached a subject neither of us wanted to touch. My dad was only sixty years old. Vigorous and in great shape, I asked what he wanted to do with the rest of his life. He obviously couldn't live with us forever. "You need to get on with your life," I said. With a glitch in my throat, I felt guilty as those words came out. I saw the same thing my dad saw in his tear-filled eyes—my mom standing on the other side of the room. But she wasn't looking on with disapproval. "I didn't lose my spouse to death," I continued. "But I lost my spouse. I'm not comparing the two at all. You and mom were together for almost forty years. But I did lose my family unit. In a very public and humiliating manner. You and mom always told me that I couldn't let it stop me from moving forward and living my life, and now I'm telling you the same thing. You can't let it stop you from living your life."

He wiped his eyes. "You need to figure out who you are, what you like, and what your interests are," I said.

He stared at me with a look of incredulity. "It sounds like you're telling me to date."

I nodded. "As hard as it is to believe, that's exactly what I'm telling you. You need to get out there. You don't have to think of it as romantic or long term. Think about it in terms of enjoying another person's company and friendship. Don't put any pressure on yourself. Don't label it. But you never know where things can go."

Several months later, he began spending time back in Oceanside. When I asked what he was up to, he was vague, providing so few details that I was reminded of the stilted conversations we had when I was a teenager trying to hide that I'd snuck out of my room the night before even though he and my mom already knew. When I pressed for information, he merely said, "I've got plans."

Okay, I thought, when he's ready to tell me, I'll be there to listen. Whatever that phase was ended, and another woman clearly began occupying his dinnertimes and weekends, and one day, as we shared coffee and a pastry in the kitchen, I finally asked, "Why are you lying to me? You act like you're doing something wrong. You aren't. I just want to know."

He looked relieved. "I wasn't sure how you and your sister would feel about it."

I took a sip of coffee. "I was the one who encouraged you to start getting out there, remember?"

My sister didn't want to hear anything about my dad's social life. She had a hard time with it, and that was partly why my dad had been vague. "Why would I tell her if it's going to hurt her?" It was surreal to have the roles flipped. At times, I felt as if I didn't have any parents left, which was simultaneously hard and weird.

But Irv Richards is an amazing dad; he was an amazing husband. He is an amazing man, who deserves to have a life, and I supported him. If I was bothered, which happened from time to time, I hid it from him, and I advised my sister to do the same. "If we have a problem, we need to deal with it and not take it to Dad," I said. "At the end of the day, we want him to be happy."

As my dad ventured into new waters, I faced some big life decisions of my own. Unable to sell my old house in the Valley, I had to decide whether to radically drop the price and take a big loss or move back in and give up the rental where we'd been living in Palisades. Since it was silly to take a financial hit on a great house whose mortgage I could afford, I returned to the house we'd left a year earlier, which meant the end of my attempt to live closer to town. As I packed, I recalled having moved more than a year earlier to put more light in my life; now, I was in such a different place in my life that I felt as if I were taking the light with me back home. Like my girls, I had a good, warm feeling when I said those words, "back home."

Familiar surroundings did not, of course, make life calm or settled. I suppose it was a sign of experience that I didn't expect anything other than more challenges and continued work. I hoped and prayed not everything coming at me would be of a seismic, life-changing level, or if it was, it would be the result of good opportunities, though as I found myself filling out school applications for Sami and arranging interviews, as well as drawing up plans to remodel my house, I realized that life was always changing, no matter what, and I'd just better get used to it. Indeed, the lessons I'd learned had enabled me to deal with and even look forward to what's around the corner.

•

PART ELEVEN

The Real Girl Next Door

1

....

BURSTING WITH PRIDE, I had tears in my eyes as I watched Sami march into the school office for an interview. Until I applied to get her into private school for kindergarten, I thought the stories I heard from other parents were exaggerated. I couldn't picture myself coaching my daughter on how to speak to an admissions administrator or fretting about what those people would think of me as they looked over her applications. My mom would've laughed at me. I was wrong.

As her interview neared, I practiced writing, reading, and spelling with her and worked both of us into a state where she didn't want to go and I thought, well, if she doesn't go, she might as well kiss her future good-bye.

Then I came to my senses. I realized nearly all the anxiety I had about her getting into this school stemmed from my fears about being judged. I was worried about what the administrators were going to think of me and her dad and how that was going to affect her. I'd worked extremely hard to protect my children from the craziness in the media surrounding Charlie and me. But watching Sami go off to be interviewed, I realized I couldn't shield them forever. Kids talked at school. They echoed their parents' conversations at home. The day would come soon enough when they'd learn how to google us. I wasn't ready for that yet. And when that day does arrive, I'm going to have to be their pillar of strength, just as they've been mine. It won't be easy for them.

Anyway, Sami got in, as did Lola later, and both times I wished I'd been able to call my mom and tell her the good news. I was able to share it with Charlie. That was also good news. Against all odds, we'd rebuilt a friendship. It seemed both improbable and impossible following the bitterness of our custody fight. But it was nice. I'll let you in on a secret. Nearly six years after we'd split, I still had moments where I was sad that we weren't a family unit. It wasn't because I still loved Charlie and wanted to be with him. No, it was about being a parent and belonging to that particular statistic. It made a part of me feel like a failure.

The part of me that wanted a sane, calm, healthy, loving, two-parent home for my children had failed. I'm simply being honest here. I had two children with Charlie, and I felt sad for them that their mom and dad didn't live together.

If that wasn't bad enough, I hated our inability to have any relationship for the sake of the girls. I sound like a broken record, but it's true. I believe it's acceptable for exes to agree to disagree and still have a relationship, and though things were hostile, something in Charlie changed and the ice began to thaw with us.

I know I'm not perfect and made mistakes during the worst of our times, and I accepted responsibility. It was so much more peaceful when he got to that place where we were able to once again have a civil conversation, and then dinner, and then be at birthday parties together.

The change happened right before Brooke gave birth to his sons. I don't know what changed in him. I can't speak for him. Whatever happened, I was relieved we could talk cordially again and spend time together. I felt as if a giant weight had been lifted.

After Charlie's boys were born, my dad and I went to see them in the hospital. I arrived straight from *Dancing with the Stars*. Although I'd changed into sweats, I was still in full hair and makeup, with lots of glitter and long lashes. I was also still filming my reality show and told the crew traveling with me that I had to make a quick stop at the hospital and they needed to turn the cameras off. Charlie took my dad and me up to the nursery, where we visited with Brooke and looked at the babies while a couple nurses stared at us with the perplexed looks of committed tabloid readers who couldn't believe the four of us were together.

"You're Denise?" one of them finally asked. I nodded. "And you have the other two children?"

I said yes.

"There are actually three moms," Charlie said.

When he walked us out, I said, "I can't even imagine what those nurses are going to say on their break." Whatever they said would be an improvement from the past few years.

Pleased, I left with lots of cute photos to show the girls, who were excited to see their new brothers. Charlie and I worked back into a nice friendship. We still had ups and downs, disagreements and periods of silence, but we worked through them on our own, and for the next two years were able to have dinners at my house with the girls, Sunday barbecues at his house with all the kids, plus birthdays and school functions. The negativity disappeared like dark clouds blown across the sky by a warm breeze that makes you want to open the windows and play outside. It was great for us and even better for the kids.

2

CUT TO CHRISTMAS 2009. I was at home when the phone rang. It was a collect call from Charlie, which I thought was odd. But he explained that he was calling from jail—and I looked across the room at Sami and Lola, reminding myself to be careful of what I said.

Charlie asked to speak with the girls; he wanted to wish them merry Christmas. Occupied with their new American Girl dolls, Sami and Lola asked if they could talk to him later. "No, you need to talk now," I said. "Daddy is in Colorado and will be skiing later. He won't have his phone on the big mountain."

Now this was probably a stupid thing to say, mostly because Charlie hates to ski, but the girls believed me and got on the phone. They had a nice conversation with their father. That's all that mattered in that moment. When I got back on, I asked if he needed any help getting out of jail. I was relieved when he said he'd made arrangements. I was already wondering how the hell I was going to get to Colorado on Christmas Day. If he'd needed help, though, I would've figured it out.

The rest of the day was surreal. I couldn't stop thinking about Charlie spending the holiday in jail. The phone rang nonstop. Later, Charlie called to let me know he was out. I heard from him again when he got home. I appreciated his checking in. I think he felt similarly about being able to count on me. By this time, I'd given up trying to make sense of our relationship. I was simply glad we were in an even better place, and it stayed that way through New Year's and into the fall.

At the end of October, I had to go to New York to do press for *Blue Mountain State*, a Spike TV series that had written me into a significant story arc. The girls, who'd grown up hearing me talk about my trips to New York, had never been there. I decided to take them and turn it into a special trip. I had been in the city for Fashion Week the month before, and designer Betsey Johnson had told me I should take the girls to the Eloise Suite at the Plaza Hotel. She'd actually decorated it herself. No more needed to be said. I splurged and booked the suite for us. Sami and Lola flipped out when I showed them the pictures online.

When I told Charlie we were going, he asked if he could come. He had a break from *Two and a Half Men*. Since we were in a stable place and I thought he was healthy at the time, I thought that I could make a nice trip even nicer for the girls. He arranged for a private jet while I canceled our commercial flight. When I told the girls their dad was also coming on the trip, they were excited. It was the first time the four of us had gone on a vacation together, ever. My publicist, Jill, nearly had a heart attack when I told her. She foresaw all the calls asking whether we were getting back together. "Don't worry about the rumors," I said. "We aren't getting back together. This is all for the girls. I think it will be a nice time."

It started out that way. After arriving in New York, we checked into the Plaza. I stayed in the parents' suite connected to my girls' room, and Charlie stayed across the hall. That first night, the four of us were tired and hung out in the pink Eloise room, had room service, and went to bed. The girls said goodnight to Charlie and walked him to his room. The next day we took the girls on a shopping spree to FAO Schwarz and the American Girl store. We also had a delicious pizza dinner at my favorite pizza restaurant, Serafina.

There, we realized this wasn't just our first trip together; it was also the first time the four of us had gone out to dinner together. Until then, we'd always eaten at one of our homes. We had a lovely time, though, then hurried across town to see *Mary Poppins* on Broadway.

The next day we went to the Museum of Natural History, which was another hit with the girls, and then back to the hotel. Charlie had dinner plans with some friends. He invited me to join them. Although my first instinct was to say no, we'd brought our nanny to watch the girls while I did my press, which meant I didn't have to worry about a babysitter. I accepted. I thought it was cool that we could go out together as friends. It showed the progress we'd made.

Charlie went to the restaurant ahead of me while I settled the girls in their room, ordered up dinner, and got myself dressed up. Once I got to the restaurant, I was ushered into a private room in the back. Charlie was at the table with three other guys, including his friend who'd traveled with us, and four attractive women who'd put themselves together for a fancy Saturday night. "By walking in here, you just confused everyone at this table, including me," Charlie joked as I sat next to him.

Soon the woman on the other side of Charlie introduced herself as Christina and asked if she could take a picture with me. "My boyfriend likes you," she said. "I'm also a fan." I thought nothing of her request as we posed together. Afterward, though, I sensed a slight awkwardness among the women at the table. I started making conversation with everyone. The man next to me said he was married with children. I assumed the woman next to him was his wife, but he corrected me, quickly adding that he wasn't going to stay long. He didn't, either.

I wondered what the hell was going on at this dinner. Then it dawned on me. I asked one of the ladies when they met the other men at the table. "Tonight," she said. Without having to ask any more questions, I knew the women were prostitutes. I looked around the table, assessing each person, as well as my place there. Okay, I thought, it's a little odd—maybe more than a little—that my ex-husband would invite me to a dinner like this. But it was, I told myself, one dinner and it was not worth making an issue out of it.

When Charlie got up from the table to go to the bathroom, Christina took his seat. Before he left, he told her, "Don't blindside Denise with what you do for a living." She replied, "I'm pretty sure she knows what we do." To be honest, though I'm a fairly nonjudgmental person, I would've preferred a dinner where I wasn't the only nonhooker among the women at the

table. I also think when you're the father of five it might be wise
to shut down that sort of behavior. But since neither of those
were the case, I will say dinner got interesting at that point.

I was genuinely curious how these women came to be at this
dinner when Charlie and I were supposed to be on a trip with
our daughters. Charlie had shared certain stories with me during
our marriage, but I had no idea how the details worked. Before
I could even ask a question, Christina said she'd learned about
the job just a few hours before dinner. She'd been shopping in
Bergdorf's when her cell phone rang. It was her "pimp" from
L.A. He asked if she could go to dinner with a client who was
in New York. "Once he mentioned it was Charlie Sheen, I said
sure, I can make it," she explained.

She told me she also had a madam in New York, had done
porn, but wanted to get out of the business, and prostitution
paid the bills. I was worried about having taken a photo with her,
since who knew where that might end up, but I relaxed when she
said her father didn't know what she did for a living. Neither did
her boyfriend, though I wondered if she even had one. If so, I'm
pretty sure he knows what she does for a living by now and, um,
same with her dad. I actually found myself in the very peculiar
situation of giving this girl advice on her boyfriend and what she
did for a living. And for a moment I thought, how in the hell
did I end up here tonight? Well, I did, so I was making the best
of it. It was one damn dinner. Even after Charlie returned from
the bathroom, the evening began to have a colorful vibe, and
like the guy who'd been next to me, I wanted to make an early
exit.

They were just starting to have an eventful evening and I

didn't want to be a buzzkill. I told Charlie that I needed to go back to the hotel. I had hair and makeup at 4:30 a.m., Howard Stern, and then an entire day of interviews. So I was going to head back while I could still get some sleep.

On the way back to the hotel, I was irked with my ex for including me in a dinner like that, never mind that we were on a trip with our daughters. I was also a little pissed at myself for having said yes and gotten myself into that situation. I had to take some responsibility. I should've asked more questions.

For the record, the picture that Christina, aka "Capri," took of us ended up on TMZ. Perhaps next time I should ask to see a résumé.

Once in the suite, I found the girls were wide-awake and watching TV. They were still on L.A. time. After I quieted them down, I climbed into bed myself; I had to get up early for my press. About an hour later, though, I was awakened by various sounds outside my door, including walkie-talkies, which is never a good sign. I opened the door and saw hotel security men knocking on Charlie's door. We had a brief conversation, the gist of which was the cops were on their way.

As soon as I heard that, I called my nanny in her room down the hall and asked her to come over to the Eloise Suite. I had a feeling I was going to need her to watch the girls. A few minutes later, the cops showed up. Several officers went into Charlie's room, and a sergeant came into mine and asked me questions about the evening. He had trouble understanding the situation, and my nonchalance confused him further.

"Now let me get this straight," he said. "You're here with your kids and your ex-husband?"

"Yes."

"Your ex-husband is staying in the room across the hall while you're in this room?"

"Yes."

"With the kids?"

"Yes."

"And you went to dinner with him and there were hookers there at the table?"

"Yes."

"And now one of the hookers is in the room across the hall with your ex-husband?"

"Yes," I said

"Where are the other hookers?"

"That I don't know."

He scratched his head. "Is there anyone in New York we can call on your ex-husband's behalf?"

"You're looking at her."

"There's no agent, manager, or lawyer?"

"Nope. They're in L.A."

After he explained what was going to happen, I quickly changed from my pajamas into jeans and a sweatshirt. Charlie was put into an ambulance, and I rode with the sergeant to the hospital, though I insisted I had to be back at 4:30 a.m. He didn't seem used to people imposing their schedules on him, but I explained I had work. Indeed, after making sure Charlie was stable and settled, the nice policeman gave me a ride back to the hotel. My nanny was awake. The girls were sound asleep, but she hadn't slept. Our eyes met and I shook my head. "I'm going to jump in the shower," I said. "Order up the biggest pot of coffee they have and a huge breakfast for both of us."

3

....

AT 5:00 A.M., my hair and makeup artist arrived. I told him about my night and asked if he thought any of it would make the news. He raised his eyebrows as if I was asking a question whose answer was so obvious. It wasn't really the brightest thing to ask, but, hey. I explained that I hadn't seen any paparazzi outside the hotel. He made the same face. "I know," I said. "I guess it's a question of when, not if."

That changed everything. The plan had been for the girls to join me after I did Howard's show. They wanted to watch me on the talk shows. I'd told them all about the studios, the sets, and the treats in the dressing rooms. But now I couldn't risk them hearing about their dad in the interviews. Once news got out about Charlie landing in the hospital after a night with hookers, and me being present, too, it was, to put it mildly, going to turn into a media shit storm. Photographers would camp outside the hotel. They'd follow me. They'd yell questions. I'd been through the drill before.

Except this time it was complicated in that we were away from home. I couldn't plant the girls in front of the TV until I got back later that night. I had to keep them occupied. If they knew what had happened, I would've pulled out of my interviews, but since they slept through the fracas I made a plan with the nanny to keep them occupied in the city while I did my job. I was proud of the show, grateful for the work, and eager to promote it. I couldn't predict what I'd face, but I'd learned a few things over the years, including how to grit my teeth, face challenges, and get through uncomfortable situations.

My interview with Howard was easy except I literally did not go to bed and actually apologized to Howard for giving a crappy interview. I have no idea what I even said, I was so distracted and, with lack of sleep, running on fumes. It was early, and news from the night before hadn't yet broken. But it was streaming across the Internet by the time I did all the other interviews. I couldn't believe the irony. Here I'd arrived in New York with no strife in my life and looking forward to doing press when I didn't have anything in my life that was off-limits. I was actually looking forward to talking about the great place I'd gotten myself to just a few months before my fortieth birthday, as well as the special trip I was on with my daughters.

But then Charlie threw that infamous dinner party. As a result, I spent nearly twelve hours telling interviewers it wasn't my place to discuss my ex and then redirecting the conversation back to my show. Later, when I met up with the girls at the hotel, I told Sami and Lola that their dad had been called back to work earlier than expected. I know I lied to them, and how I was able to keep a lid on everything I have no idea. But given their ages, I felt it was the best strategy. After more interviews the next day, we headed back home. I stayed in the car while my nanny brought the girls outside. I felt terrible for not being able to say good-bye to the Eloise Suite with them, but photographers and media vans were camped outside the hotel and it would've been a mess if we'd walked out together.

Despite the way that trip ended, I didn't let it affect my relationship with Charlie. In Charlie's eyes at the time, I could do no wrong. He treated me like a champ. For all the assistance I'd provided that drama-filled night in New York, he referred to me as his MVP. From such a big sports fan as him, I knew that was a serious compliment. He also said that I was finally getting the respect I deserved. After everything we'd been through, that compliment meant a lot.

For the next few months, I was involved with my busy home life. My days were packed with school activities and playdates for the girls, going on auditions, building my Web presence, and starting a remodel on my house. Not everything worked. I even let a friend talk me into going on a blind date with a chiropractor. He sent me a text offering to come over and give me an "adjustment" in exchange for a glass of wine. When I didn't respond, he sent me a picture of himself shirtless, holding a beer. That was supposed to impress me? Sorry. The blind date never happened—and neither will any other blind dates!

Shortly after the holidays, Charlie called to invite the girls and me to go with him to Las Vegas. I politely declined, which earned me a call from his friend. "I'll leave my phone on at night in case something happens," I said with a knowing laugh. He said, "Okay, D.R."

Nothing happened that needed *my* attention. But everything else happened, according to reports. Charlie met a girl who was later introduced to the world as one of his "goddesses," and his weekend ended up on the news. As the star of TV's top-rated sitcom, Charlie's behavior was irresistible to the media. They raised the same red flags that I worried about in private. I did my best to make sure the girls remained unaware of the reports. While I could turn off the TVs at certain hours, making sure they didn't hear *Access Hollywood* or *Entertainment Tonight*, I couldn't control what kids said to them at school, and with so much attention on Charlie, kids heard their parents talking at home and brought that back to the playground.

Unfortunately, between the lies I was telling the girls, their dad's erratic behavior, and bits and pieces they heard on the news or at school, I needed to have a difficult conversation with them. I'd always planned to speak to them about addiction, but I'd hoped to put it off till they were older. I also had to figure out what the hell to say.

Well, I wasn't going to shut the door on Charlie or wait till the girls were teenagers to tell them the truth. I couldn't. They were destined to find out sooner rather than later.

I followed my gut, and in mid-January 2011, my heart told me it was time to start explaining things. After researching the subject, I bought a book written to help children understand their parents' addiction. I picked what I thought was a good time and sat Sami and Lola down on the sofa in our family room and began to read the book. Halfway through, I started to tear up. Lola closed the book and said, "Mom, you don't have to read this."

I apologized for being upset and dried my eyes. "Yes, I do," I said. "This is hard for Mommy to explain, but I want to read it to you." I started again, made it through the entire story, and looked at the girls sitting quietly next to me. Sami was leaning against me on one side and Lola had her hand on my left on the other. Any doubts I had about whether they understood the book were eased when Lola looked up at me and said, "Now how do we help Daddy?"

Good question. "I don't know," I said. "But when Daddy gets help, we will support him."

She thought for a minute. "How will Daddy get help?"

Plenty of people were asking the same thing. "Me and some of Daddy's friends are trying to figure that out," I said.

4

....

A FEW DAYS later I visited Charlie. I was concerned about his behavior, as were others in his life. I explained that I'd read a book to the girls to help them understand him better. I also said that I hoped he realized all of his children needed him to be healthy. "I'm not judging you, this is your life," I said. "I'm just being honest. And right now I'm worried about you."

Thanking me, and reassuring me he was okay, he told me of his plan to move four women into his home. They'd be his girlfriends—his "porn family," as he called it. I could see how a young guy in his twenties might fantasize about having several girlfriends living with him, but at forty-five years old and with five children? I had trouble comprehending this. My heart sank as he explained that it had taken him a while to find the right group of women, but he finally had the four picked out. He also wanted me to move into the neighborhood with him and his new family, saying he'd buy me a new place down the street.

Although as quickly as he made that offer on the house, he took it away. Which was fine; I had no intention of moving there.

I shook my head, trying to hide my sadness, not to mention my fear the girls might be losing him. "I can't even begin to explain that to our daughters," I said quietly. He said, "Tell them their dad marches to his own beat."

The next morning I was walking into the theater at Sami's school to watch her sing in a class performance. My phone rang. Charlie was in the hospital. I barely made it through Sami's performance without bawling. Between the pride I had for my daughter and the concern I had for her father, I was a mess. Things were starting to come to a head for me. I'd proven I can be strong and put on a brave face in almost any situation, but I was mad and upset that I had to do it over and over. Constantly lying to our kids, covering things up, making excuses, pretending things were okay when they were not. I started asking myself why I felt the need to navigate everything on my own. I kept asking myself, "Why does their dad have to live such an outrageous life?"

Then I reminded myself, I can't change Charlie. He is merely being himself. He never professed to be anyone else. I tried to be philosophical, as is the only option in such circumstances. You don't have to ignore the roiling emotions that come with upsets and disappointments, but as I learned time and time again, you can't crumble, either. For whatever reason, Charlie and I are on a journey together. We created two magnificent lives, and therefore we are going to be in each other's lives forever. Instead of flying off the handle and making judgments on him, I keep moving forward. Quite frankly, I've learned my opinion doesn't matter a lot of the time, so why make our relationship more volatile and chaotic?

I don't see any sense in stressing about things I can't change or control. Charlie is on his own path, and this is the lifestyle he has chosen. That doesn't mean I condone it, but I've learned to accept it. And despite the roller coaster of being up and down, one thing I know for sure: I'll always be there for Charlie. From the time we split, I've been determined to have a relationship with him, and I'm not giving up. It's about our kids and it's important for them that I soldier on.

We have had one of the worst divorces in Hollywood; that's not something I'm proud of. If we can get to a place that's peaceful, then anyone can. It's not easy, and again, I think it's okay to agree to disagree a lot. But when you do disagree, put aside your argument and let the kids know that they come first, and they are loved. Show up at birthday parties, school functions, lessons, recitals, games, and holiday dinners together. I've learned to suck it up. It ain't about you anymore, it's about the kids. That's the mantra I live by.

It's not easy. Believe me. Charlie has a sharp tongue, and when we disagree, I'm on the receiving end of some pretty colorful speeches. Sometimes it's hard to let his insults roll off my back. But I do. In his defense, he often accuses me of being unreasonable when I turn into protective mother hen. He says I shelter the girls too much. Maybe I do. I don't care. At times his lifestyle veers in colorful directions, and I don't want the girls around it. I'm stubborn and not afraid to stand up to him no matter how angry he gets. As I've said, even when we aren't on the best of terms, I have faith we'll get back to a good place. We've done it before, and we'll continue to find our way back again when necessary.

At the end of February, I was at a table in the Beverly Hills Four Seasons Hotel, working on the above paragraph, when my phone was flooded with news that CBS and Warner Bros. had just suspended production of *Two and a Half Men* for the rest of the season. I wasn't surprised. After several weeks of Charlie's sharing his negative opinions on the show's executive producer and the network on TV, in print, on the radio, and over the Internet, the network and the studio had had enough. Two weeks later, they fired him altogether.

Nothing he said subsequently on talk shows, the radio, and even in an interview streamed live on the Internet from his backyard surprised me. I've been asked how I am handling this all lately, but the reality is I've been handling this on and off for seven years. The truth is: This is not the man that I married; this is the man that I divorced. What did surprise me was how very public Charlie wanted his thoughts to be. It breaks my heart. He's an amazing actor, with the capacity to be an amazing person and father. It hurts to see him like this.

I believed, and continue to believe, he'll get through this. If he doesn't, then, sadly, perhaps tragically, he doesn't. It's up to him. Either way, I'm resigned to many long talks with my girls. Whatever Charlie's differences and conflicts, though, I will always be here for him.

He's bashed me on his Torpedo of Truth World Tour. I know what you're thinking. I know. What can I say that I haven't already said? That's life with Charlie. It's up and down. Being around someone with an addiction as deep as Charlie's is painful to see and hurtful to experience in person. I guess I have thick skin and a big, understanding heart. I also know at the end of the day he is the father of my daughters and I need to maintain a relationship, only in the healthiest sense, for them.

As I look back, Charlie's past should probably have been a giant red flag when we met. Maybe I was naïve or so in love I looked at him, and us, through rose-colored glasses. Whatever it was, I made a choice and it took me on this wild and crazy journey of ours. Not only did Charlie give me the best gifts anyone could ever give, my daughters, he's also proven to be the best teacher I've ever had, and for that, I thank him. I've learned a lifetime of lessons from him, and I'm still learning. That doesn't mean I'm always clear on what I've learned. I'm not. It takes time to see the good come to light out of the bad. But eventually things make sense.

I wish I could tie everything up in a neat little bow. I can't. At the moment I'm writing this sentence, we aren't in the best place. But I'm counting on that to change. While he's splattering the world with tiger blood, I will ride out this tumultuous wave, hoping for the calm to be restored. When it's peaceful, well, I will cherish those moments without knowing or worrying how long the peace will last. I navigate this as best as I can. I make mistakes. I learn. I try my best.

As always, I'm rooting for him. It means the best for us.

5

....

AT THE NADIR of Charlie's implosion, I turned forty. I celebrated with an amazing dinner party with my closest friends in Los Angeles, but I spent my actual birthday in New York following a taping of *The View*. I'd guest-hosted on the show's "Third Annual Mutt Show." Not only did I survive Barbara's queries about Charlie, I left the studio with Chocolate Chip, a two-year-old terrier mix we later named Coco. What a whirlwind she experienced, going from a year in a shelter to a night at the Ritz-Carlton, where she celebrated my birthday with me. What a story she heard me tell her that night.

It's funny. You think about milestones like a fortieth birthday, read about them in magazines, discuss them with friends, worry about their significance, plan elaborate celebrations to distract yourself from fears about aging, and then, as in my case, you find yourself on the big day after having dinner with friends in New York alone in a hotel room with a strange terrier, realizing these events we build into mountains are only as important as we make them. I don't want to diminish the significance of the day itself. Turning forty was a big deal. But how I felt about turning forty was much more important than the actual day itself, and I'll tell you what. I felt pretty good.

I don't look at forty and say, "Oh my God, I'm getting old." No, I think of it more in terms of someone whose mother died at fifty-three. And my mom's dad died at fifty-three. I struggled with those kinds of fears, not whether my face is going to sag or my boobs will hit my knees. My job is to make sure I'm around to see my kids grow up.

On the major plus side—and I hate that this sounds cliché—but I feel as if, at forty, I've arrived at a new beginning. Emotionally and physically, I feel better now than I did in my twenties. I'm more optimistic, too—and I was a positive-looking person then. The reason? I know who I am, and I'm comfortable with that. I'm in a good place. The stuff I worried about in my twenties and thirties rolls off my back. If someone had asked me ten or fifteen years ago where I saw myself at this age, I would've said happily married, with four children, and making a movie every year. My mom wouldn't have been gone, either. But I'm not disappointed or defeated by where I am at; in fact, I'm philosophical about it. I have a good sense of what matters, what *really* matters. I feel capable, smarter, and wiser, and pleasantly eager to find out what's next.

I'd love to get remarried. But I could have a serious someone with me for a long, long time without walking down the aisle again. He just needs to be the right person. He also has to know something: I won't ever get divorced again. Ever. If we were to split, he'd have to get a house next door or on the same block. I'd also like to have more children. Definitely. But who the hell can say if that will happen? All I know for sure is that I'm not putting my life on hold.

I can feel my mom's approval. She was clearly taken too soon, but the part of me that thinks in a spiritual sense believes that we all arrive with a purpose, and I think she fulfilled hers. I sense it in me every day. Maybe that's part of a purpose all of us share. We're supposed to pass on the best part of us. According to my mom, I was always a nurturer, as was she, whether it was with people or animals. We're similar that way. Just walk into my house and you'll know. You'll see the kids, all their stuff, and you'll be overrun by dogs. If you could only hear the yapping right now, predinner, and Lola and Sami running up to me to show me pictures they drew.

I've been involved in animal rescue for quite some years. When my mom's dog, Sheena, passed away, I called a friend who worked at the Best Friends Animal Society and said I wanted to adopt a dog nobody wanted. They showed me two, and I ended up with a Chihuahua mix that was blind in one eye. He lost the sight in his other eye soon after I brought him home. His name is Preston. And he's a sweetie. There was another dog there—a black one who looked like a sausage with four squat legs. After I brought Preston home, I couldn't stop thinking of that black dog, so I decided I'd foster him. Although he was full of energy at my house, they said he was depressed in the cage at adoption events when they took him back. As soon as I heard that, I made room for him in the household, too. Soon I heard about a dog with two legs that were deformed from abuse. He was about to be put down. We found a bed for him and named him Scooter. His operations cost four grand per leg, but I'll tell you what, he's the sweetest dog of the bunch. He was worth it. I think rescue dogs are the most grateful animals I've been around. They show you that gratefulness day in and day out.

I'm often asked why I'm into rescuing pets. I don't have a simple answer, but periodically at night as we're all going to sleep, most of the dogs in their own bed, except my French bull-dog, Hank, who often curls up on my bed, and a couple that bunk with the girls, I've come to understand, even if I can't put it concisely into words, that I get as much, if not more, out of it than they do. Caring for them is about constantly reminding us about the responsibility we have to nurture and care for creatures other than ourselves. At the end of the day, we all just want to feel loved.

It's a good message, a good lesson.

I have a group of close-knit girlfriends, and we meet once a month at someone's home for dinner. We call ourselves the supper club. All of us are moms, and all of us are in the business. We spend the night talking about everything, and I mean everything, knowing that nothing we say leaves that room. It's liberating to share private thoughts and discover you aren't the only one who's ever had them. We support one another, whether it's tweeting about someone's TV series or movie, or just getting up from the table and giving someone a hug. The cornerstone of faith is knowing that if you fall, you can count on someone to pick you up, and I have that with family and friends.

If anyone reading this book is going through a tough time, I hope I've given you reason to believe that there is light at the end of the dark tunnel. There is. Whether you've gotten divorced, lost a loved one, or are struggling to find a job and make ends meet, whatever the challenge is, know that you can fight the fight and get to a better place if you follow what's really important. I won't tell you what's important. We all know. It's already inside us. And as for how you go about it, remember that you can't change other people. We can only change how we respond to situations and people and ultimately who we want to be.

•

At the end of March 2011, my beloved dog Lucy died from liver cancer. She was the first dog I cared for as an adult. She was at my side through everything and everyone for eleven years: through every relationship, every crisis, every birth of a child, every tragedy, and every triumph. She was a huge part of my life, and it was tough letting her go. But you know what? Life goes on—at least in my house.

The other night Lola asked me how babies got into the stomach. Before I could answer, Sami, who overheard her sister's question, jumped onto the sofa and said, "I don't even want to know. I have a feeling it's gross!"

I laughed.

I made a note to tell my dad and Charlie.

It's easy to get lost in the meaningless distractions we're made to believe are important when, as I've learned, the keys to the life we want are in our hands. We make the decisions that affect our future. As I sit here contemplating everything I've been through, I'm wondering what advice I would give myself if I could go back in time, pre-Charlie. One thing I wouldn't tell myself is to do anything differently. I don't have regrets—not when I look at my daughters. They have been my strength, inspiring me to be strong, optimistic, and better. In general, I don't believe in regrets. People make mistakes. Life is what it is at the moment. Make the best of it. That's the advice I'd give myself if I could go back in time. Be patient. My mom liked to say, "This, too, shall pass." She was right. When I was younger, I used to worry about what was going to happen the next month, the next year, or what I was going to do in two years. Now, I live in the moment, and try to enjoy it more. Life is too short to do otherwise. You never know what's going to happen next. It doesn't help to worry about all the crap in the past. Nor can you comprehend all the what-ifs in the future. If the risks you want to take feel right, take them. Be selfless. Be loving. Keep your heart open.

In life, you need thick skin. You can't give a shit about what other people are going to say. As I learned, all you can do is be your authentic self. If you want to make changes in your life, start with baby steps. Give yourself achievable goals. Go for a walk if you want exercise. If you need company, get girlfriends together. If you need friends, organize drinks with coworkers. If you don't like the way you look, start with a new hairdo. Most important, don't procrastinate. Don't invent excuses. And don't give up if things don't work out the way you want the first time. Life is all about trial and error. Be fearless. It's worked for me.

As I said much earlier, when I turned thirty, a friend of mine promised the best was still ahead of me. It was hard to believe, but I'm beginning to think she was right. Indeed, Oprah Winfrey is another who is always saying life gets better with age. Judging from the way I feel and the turns in my life, I've chosen to believe her. I am forty. I feel great. I feel fortunate. I feel hopeful. With all I've been through, I feel empowered. I also feel smarter than I was twenty years ago, and even sexier. In a way, life is just beginning, though maybe you can feel that at any age.

I've never been someone who has to have a boyfriend or to be in a relationship, but I still want one. I would like to meet Mr.

Right and get remarried (for life, of course!), make plans, and end up in a rocking chair on a porch looking out at a passel of grandchildren. I'm ready for my next journey and I think that's a great way to feel.

I hope from reading this you've discovered I'm a lot like you. I think most of us share the same thoughts and aspirations. At heart, I'm a simple Midwestern girl who got swept up in a life I never dreamed possible. I've had amazing experiences, friendships, and loves, but with them came periods of grief and trials. For all the highs and lows, life evens out. I make my children my top priority, I try to help my dad, and I put family at the center of my life. I get involved in causes. That's about all anyone can do in life. You face each day. You try your best. The crises I've navigated are not unique, which is partly why I wrote this book. If you're going through similar challenges, I hope you're able to find strength and comfort from my story, if only from learning that you aren't alone. All of us are part of a community where we can support each other. If you don't believe me, find me through my website or Twitter. I'm there for you, just as so many of you have been there for me. I would've loved for my girls to grow up beyond the spotlight of famous parents and a father who's made explaining divorce even more complicated. But what better skill to teach than resiliency? The message I want to leave you with?

Keep looking forward.

And stay real.

ACKNOWLEDGMENTS

....

I'd like to thank all the people in my life who have loved me unconditionally and stuck by me through the ups and downs on this journey.

SAMI AND LOLA: You are my angels, my pillars of strength; I love you both so much. Thank you for letting me see the world through your beautiful eyes. You are my biggest accomplishment; you complete me.

ELOISE: My little angel; I'm so blessed you chose us.

NELLIE: Thank you for being the best sister I could ever have. You keep it real with me and keep me completely grounded.

MY DAD: Thank you for your love, support, and teaching me from an early age to take risks. Thank you for being the best dad and grandpa in the world.

ALEC: I'm so proud of the path you're on and the young man you're becoming.

KIM: We've been through so many years together. Thank you for all the memories and for always being there.

NATALIE: My British bestie . . . thank you for pushing me to write this book and for your friendship.

CHUCK JAMES: I'll never forget the day we met. Thank you for being so passionate and for all your hard work. You have been there for me not only as my agent but also as a dear friend through thick and thin. During the ups and downs you've always been very encouraging and have never given up on me. I can't thank you enough for believing in me and not dropping me during the worst time of my life.

JILL FRITZO AND AME VAN IDEN: Thank you for all the work you do; you go above and beyond.

PAUL VERHOEVEN AND JOHN MCNAUGHTON: Thank you for giving me my first part in a movie—it changed my life. I can't thank you enough for believing in me, that I could live up to your vision. I'll never forget the experience I had with you both; truly, I'm so grateful.

LOUIS: For teaching me how to dance and becoming a dear friend in the process.

KELLY CARLSON: My gorgeous friend. Thank you for your support and friendship. You are a true friend and even more beautiful on the inside.

SUZI KALTMAN: Thank you for always being there for me. I cherish our friendship, mama!

MINDY WEISS: Not only are you the most magnificent event planner, you're the most amazing friend. Thanks for being there from the beginning. . . . Love u, Min!

PAT (SCHWEETBABE): Where do I start? Thank you, I'll love you forever . . . xo.

CHARLIE: Through it all . . . I can't thank you enough for the two most precious gifts anyone has ever given me.

JACK: Thank you for being there when I needed you most.

MY SUPPER CLUB GIRLS: Ali S., Ali L., Lisa R., Nancy O., Brooke B., Holly P., Tori S., Candace B., I love our dinners so much . . . thanks for the support and friendship. I always look forward to the next potluck.

TODD GOLD: My new neurotic friend . . . I think you know more about me than pretty much anyone. Thank you for being patient during this process and putting up with my stubbornness. I'm so proud of what we've done. Thank you.

DAN STRONE, MY LITERARY AGENT: Thank you for taking me on and believing in this book.

JEN BERGSTROM, KARA CESARE, AND JEN ROBINSON: I can't thank you enough for publishing my book and believing in my story and allowing me to express my voice.

MY TWITTER FOLLOWERS: Thank you for your love and support and for inspiring me to write this book.

MY MOM: Thank you for being my rock and being my biggest fan and supporter. You've taught me so many beautiful lessons. I hope to be half the mom you are. Not a day goes by that I don't think about you. I love you and miss you dearly.

I love you all and thank you from the bottom of my heart . . . xoxo, Denise